If you're feeling lost, take a walk in the woods.

—Joelle Chase, friend

God in the Yard

spiritual practice for the rest of us

a 12-week course in
discovery and playing towards God

l. l. barkat

 T. S. Poetry Press

T. S. Poetry Press
Ossining, New York

The scripture quotations contained herein are from the New Revised
Standard Version Bible, copyright © 1989 by the Division of Christian
Education of the National Council of the Churches of Christ in the U.S.A.
Used by permission. All rights reserved. Quotations of the Psalms are taken
from THE MESSAGE. Copyright © by Eugene H. Peterson, 1993, 1994,
1995, 1996, 2000, 2001, 2002. Used by Permission of NavPress, All Rights
Reserved. www.navpress.com (1-800-366-7788)

PlayDoh is a registered trademark of the Hasbro Company. Ipod is a
registered trademark of Apple Computer.

Some names in this text have been changed to preserve privacy.

Cover image: Kelly Langner Sauer. www.kellylangnersauer.com

ISBN 978-0-9845531-1-2

Library of Congress Cataloging-in-Publication Data:
Barkat, L.L.
        [Non-fiction, spiritual.]
        God in the Yard:
        spiritual practice for the rest of us/L.L. Barkat
        ISBN 978-0-9845531-1-2
        Library of Congress Control Number: 2010927333

To my online community,
whose encouragement and insights
helped bring this work into being

Contents

Before You Start

This is the story of an unusual year, when I did something I never intended to do. But it is also a course in *discovery* and *playing towards God*, through spiritual practice, offered with gentle expectations. You'll be given options like free writing, writing response, physical and mental play, blogging (or alternatives).

Choose what works. You can take your time and do all that's offered, pick only a few things to try, or simply read. The journey is yours.

Find a single
tree, find
the moon.
It doesn't
take much.
Just begin.

Woods: invitation • week I

When I was a child, I lived in the woods.

Not literally, of course. I wasn't a pint-sized Paul Bunyan, wielding my axe, toddling around with a stuffed blue ox. The woods were a place I sought solace from a difficult life. There, I watched the creek change from a silver-green ribbon, to amber lace, from ice-blue to spring's rush and tumble of white. I floated sticks and made pine needle beds. Sometimes I raced my sister across the rocks, then knocked her into the reeds. In the woods I was free.

Today, the squeal of a garbage truck wakes me three times a week. Horns and sirens break through the quiet of dawn and night. My house clings to the edge of a hill less than a quarter of an acre in size, and a rusty chain-link fence hitches my yard to the yards of my neighbors. Three unidentified cats use my front steps to nap and my back yard to poop. My sister lives far away.

There is a part of me that feels pinched in this life—a life I freely chose when I put distance between me and my growing-up place. But it's no fun to live with the pain of pinching. That is why I first returned to the woods.

~

---

1. And you?

In your journal, or during a small-group sharing time, complete the thoughts:

"When I was a child, I lived..."
"Today I live..."
"If I could, I would return to..."

It might be an exaggeration to call the trees in my back yard *woods*. A single fir spreads her arms above a patch of English ivy. Two maples reach to the sun. Wood-winged bushes and thorns tussle in the shade. This is a very small space, an "edge" if you will.

Technically, an edge is where one habitat meets another—where grass gradually gives way to bushes, which gives way to trees, or vice versa. I saw this recently, on a trip south. A sign explained the vitality of these regions, "Edges are places that support a broad range of wildlife." The bald eagle is an example of a bird who lives in the edge; he nests in tall pine trees, but he fishes in wetlands and marshes.

Culturally, we're not trained to love edges, but might they hold something unseen, unexpected? I think about Wendell Berry's trip to Peru, where he saw mountain farmers grow food in small, seemingly inhospitable places. He says, "... those fields hold their soil on those slopes, first of all, by being little. By being little they protect themselves against erosion, but their smallness also permits attention to be focused accurately and competently on the details."

Smallness permits attention. The fields stay intact because they are little. Could I find something worthwhile in my little back yard? Berry seemed to suggest it was possible.

Around the time I considered his words, a friend expressed surprise that I'd never read *Radical Simplicity*, a book by Jim Merkel, about living with limits. Well, I was feeling limited. Not just with my tiny yard space, but also in my professional development.

An extended writing project had left me feeling oddly empty. It stirred a longing for those big woods of long ago, made me covet childhood walks and lazy afternoons of tracing sticks in the mud. It also created a sense of professional discontent. I wanted more time to focus. No more of this writing-on-the-edge-of-a-napkin. I wanted to go to exotic places to jumpstart my creativity. I needed an Annie Dillard-style trip to the Galapagos. But, quite simply, I was going nowhere.

I ordered *Radical Simplicity*.

Saying, "I ordered," implies some kind of control. But I have doubts. Merkel's book arrived in my life with rather suspicious timing. This suggests there is a divine librarian who puts things on hold at the library, for people who need a particular book at a particular time.

That is just a theory.

As it turned out, Merkel's book would jumpstart a commitment I had no plans of making. I would be compelled to do what Berry said the Peruvian farmers do: focus accurately and competently on the details. The details of what? I had no idea.

The invitation was simple: find a secret spot somewhere in nature, go there for an hour every day, open your ears and eyes and fingertips and take it all in, journal if you want. Make sure the spot is within walking distance. Do it for a year.

I have children. I home educate these children. This is a great investment of energy. I am a work-at-home professional. I need space in my day to research exotic trips to the Galapagos. I don't have time to sit with the squirrels.

Plus, the only secret spot in nature within walking distance is the edge of my yard. If my neighbors want to, they can watch me look at the clouds, while they make fish sticks and pick the day's Play-Doh® off their kitchen tables. Maybe they will turn me in to the time-management police. And, besides, grown people don't sit in an excuse-for-a-woods, especially not in snow or rain or blistering heat, especially not on a red plastic sled with a yellow pull rope.

That is what I said to myself before I pulled a kiddie sled through the edge of a sub-zero day.

---

2. And you?

In your journal, or during a small-group sharing time, complete the thoughts:

"A small space I tend to overlook is..."
"In order to grow, I feel like I need..."
"If I could, I would go..."

Vinita Hampton Wright says that creative work is an "event and a partnership," which begins in a place we hardly understand. It is important to have faith in this place, which she calls the soul. Mostly she applies this wisdom to creative processes like writing a book or a poem, but I think her wisdom can also describe the creative process of spiritual growth.

She says, "Think of it this way. Not only is your soul bigger and wiser than you are, it knows the story better than you do too. You may begin a poem and think you know where it's going, but you're going on your conscious, limited knowledge. Your well contains the true end of the poem, and you simply won't know it until your creativity draws it up... just do what comes to you, and you watch what appears."

So, regardless of what the neighbors might think, I went outside... to sit with intruder cats, drink green tea and read the Psalms, to commune with creation and find some contentment and beauty.

In choosing to do this, was my soul bigger and wiser than I? Maybe it would collude with the Divine in an event and a partnership the Psalmist speaks of this way: "You get us ready for life: you probe our soft spots, you knock off our rough edges" (Ps. 7:9)

Or maybe I would just freeze my butt off in winter and get tick bites in summer. You never can tell with these things.

---

3. And you?

In your journal, or during a small-group sharing time,
complete the thoughts:
"If I commit to going to some kind of 'small space' (outdoors,
my journal, a small group, a dance or art class), I'm afraid that..."
"I shouldn't bother with 12 weeks of this, because..."
"I believe (or do not believe) my soul is bigger and wiser than I,
because..."

Playing towards God & discovery

I'm not sure when this whole business of spiritual practice became so serious. Maybe it traces back to Benedict's Rule of Life, which ordered the lives of monks around prayer, study and work. Once, I read that Benedict himself was not the type you'd expect to see on the playground.

Maybe he never read Proverbs 8. Or perhaps it was due to his serious bible translation. Wisdom is playful, but some texts frame her words, "When he established the heavens, I was there, when he drew a circle on the face of the deep...then I was beside him, like a master worker..."

Benedict shouldn't be judged too harshly. I never noticed the playful attitude of Wisdom, until one day when I read the footnote; "master worker" can also be translated "little child." Have you seen a little child, delighting in something he loves? The sense is far different from a master worker, which elicits visions of toil and exclusionary concentration. ("Shoo! Don't bother me, I'm working on a universe!")

When I could see Wisdom dodging God's feet, chanting singsong, clapping hands, this radically changed my view of God's invitations. Unlike Benedict's Rule, which seemed to order me into spiritual life, God in this particular passage seemed to call me to play.

But we needn't rely on a single passage. Biblical festivals have classically included elements of play. At Passover, for instance, the youngest child asks four questions, one from each of four types of children—the wise, the wicked, the simple, and one who does not know how to ask the right questions. Through a child's role-play, adults become like children, and enter the grace of celebration.

I also like to remember that *play*, though it engages our senses and calls us to enactment, is not limited to light-hearted topics. My children tell me they had a war in their woods—one so traumatic they responded by creating a kind of governance system. Another time I saw my girls and their friend in the back yard; I wondered why the neighbor child was lying so still. "We're having her funeral," my children explained.

Christianity's sister faith Judaism is filled with this kind of play: reenacting Passover, sitting shiva after a death and later leading the bereaved down his driveway to symbolically reenter society... these are forms of play that lead us out of ourselves and restore us to God and community.

Kent Ira Groff notes, "To restore the soul is to renew the healthy child in us, awake with all the senses.... We cannot DO the restoring; we can only train the eye of awareness, the fingers of expression, and the figures of speech." However, our spiritual goal is not simply to renew the child but to play through the child, towards soul restoration, towards a Proverbs-style partnership between us and God, preparing the way for grace in the world.

To encourage the eye of awareness, fingers of expression, figures of speech, Groff recommends attention to nine play areas:

- **linguistic verbal** – words, sounds and signs
- **logical/mathematical** – numbers, puzzlers; toy with ideas
- **spatial/visual** – images, shapes, space, imagination
- **musical/rhythmic** – drums, strings, tones, rhymes, puns
- **kinesthetic/bodily** – dance, sport, drama and mime
- **interpersonal** – games, jokes, tricks, humor and songs
- **intrapersonal** – dreams, musings, insights, and Ahas!
- **naturalist** – birds, trees, water, stars, wonder, and cycles of birth/decay
- **existentialist** – play with "why" questions like a two-year-old

Throughout the 12 weeks of exploration, I've tried to provide options based on the nine areas above. Where I've been remiss, you might take up the challenge. If something feels strange, you can skip it. Or decide, like I did when I pulled my kids' sled to the back yard, that maybe it's time to do things a little differently... and who cares if the neighbors see.

Can you be like Wisdom the Child, opening yourself to God's creative possibilities? Why not? I bet you could use a break from the same old, same old. Come on, try it. Come and play.

Week 1 prayer

Father, Son and Holy Spirit, join me in play, as I begin a journey of discovery that entwines knowledge of myself and knowledge of You.

Sabbath on the page

At least several times this week (or every day if you can swing it), try resting on the page by engaging in stream-of-consciousness writing (otherwise known as free writing). The point is not to make a point, but to release your thoughts without judging them. You want them to move freely. Freedom in thinking can be a form of prayer, and over time it can relax you and give you new directions and insights you never expected.

Blog it, to process and share

It's the end of week one. Consider blogging about your experience. If you don't blog, you can do a "week-in-review" in your journal or write a letter to a friend or God. You could include:

- An idea that was new to you, or a quote you appreciated
- Something you liked about your experience
- Something you felt anxious or unsure about
- Any questions you have (no need to answer them; sometimes the ask-

ing is the most important step)

• Things you were reminded of: a story, memory, piece of art or music, bible verse or prayer, poem, current or historical event

Rules: the way • week 2

*In the end, this is the most hopeful thing any of us can say
about spiritual transformation:* **I cannot transform myself,** *or
anyone else for that matter. What I can do is create the conditions
in which spiritual transformation can take place...*

— Ruth Haley Barton

I've always liked cardinals. Vibrant splashes that adorn white pine and maple. They delight me with their brilliant presence. Mostly. I say this because I remember the day I thought my back yard cardinals had turned into Hitchcock's *The Birds*.

It happened at the edge of the little woods. I was minding my own business, picking up sticks, pulling weeds, when a birdy scream interrupted my rhythm. A male cardinal flew straight towards me, then wheeled back to a branch above and continued its tirade. My heart beat fast. My palms started sweating.

I watched the angry bird without moving. Then I heard another scream, pitched differently, coming from the small trees further back. A female cardinal, mousy brown with bare blushes of red, had joined the attack. What had possessed this aggressive couple?

Then I heard it. In the lulls between their screams, I heard the softer sound of "shrip, shrip, shripping" coming from somewhere near my feet. Ivy and pine needles shifted, rustled. A tiny round brown puff emerged. Their baby.

Julian of Norwich, a passionate medieval mystic, would have understood the protective instincts of my back yard cardinals. She says of God, "... he showed me something small, no bigger than a hazelnut, lying in the palm of my hand... and it was as round as a ball.... I was amazed that it could last, for I thought that because of its littleness it would suddenly have fallen into nothing.... In this little thing I saw three properties. The first is that God made it, the second is that God loves it, the third is that God preserves it...."

What Julian doesn't explain is the paradoxical nature of this creation, love and preservation. Similar to the thorny issue of psychological nature-versus-nurture, our spiritual selves seem to have two sides: God-given, loved and protected versus self/other-given, loved, and protected.

So on the one hand there is Psalm 139:13, "Oh, yes, you shaped me first inside, then out; you formed me in my mother's womb..." suggesting God's control over our being. And on the other hand, we find stories like Josiah's, a good man who ultimately lost his life when "he did not listen to the words of Neco from the mouth of God, but joined battle in the plain of Megiddo" (2 Chron. 35:22).

In other words, spiritual growth and health is complicated by the question of whose job it is to keep our lives from falling into nothing. If we believe the whole matter rests in God's hands, we can sleep like Rip Van Winkle and wake up whole on the other side; we can rest like a tiny hazelnut in the palm of life and trust that all will be well.

Conversely, if we believe the matter rests squarely in our hands, we might crush ourselves with the weight of discipline in an effort to put ourselves together—much like the young Karen Armstrong. She describes in *The Spiral Staircase* a rigid spiritual journey in the nunnery that plunged her into depression and physical illness (not that all such cloister journeys are like this, but hers was).

Or we could walk to the edge of an ordinary day and watch the birds.

---

1. And you?

In your journal, or during a small-group sharing time,

complete the thoughts:

"I have (do not have) quiet spaces, openings in my day, to let myself simply drift, so God can come alongside me. They look like (I wish they looked like)... "
"I think people can (cannot) change, because..."
"I believe it is my job (God's job) to preserve my soul, because..."

I've heard it said that when it's time for baby birds to fly, their no-non-sense mamas knock them out of the nest. Maybe some fledgling some-where must put up with such heavy-handed (or beaked?) techniques. But I recently learned from an avian specialist that for most baby birds it comes to a matter of internal readiness. Feathers grow long, muscles grow strong, bodies plump up, and it's time. The baby walks out ready to try her wings. Sometimes she makes her way, branch by branch, down to the ground. Or she might dive like an Olympic hopeful, gliding a bit if she's lucky, or enduring a crash landing if the breeze doesn't quite go her way.

The day I found that baby cardinal "shrriping" in the undergrowth, she'd obviously left home, maybe for the first time— fully exposed to the likes of me, to the squirrels (should they care) and to the neighborhood cats (who surely would have cared, had they known. Trust me on this, I have more than once found a cat-mauled bird hidden in the grass).

It seemed really important that the baby learn to fly. And if that baby had any doubts, papa and mama screeching and diving must have pro-vided incentive and urgency.

Around the time I began my year of outdoor solitude, I felt an ur-gency inside. Some people had gotten unhappy with me. They said things I didn't know how to interpret. Were they right? I felt like a fail-ure. The feelings went so deep they affected me physically. My limbs felt heavy. My heart felt squeezed. I cried more than usual and vacillated between anger (*damn the world!*) and morbid fantasies (*what if I just happened to drive off this bridge?*). Did I need to learn, yet again, to fly?

---

2. And you?

In your journal, or during a small-group sharing time, complete the thoughts:

"I believe that 'failure to fly' is (is not) dangerous because... "
"The last time someone told me something negative about myself, I responded by..."
"When I experience deep emotions that swing from one extreme to the other, I think this might mean ..."

Adele Calhoun's *Spiritual Disciplines Handbook*, which features about 65 different practices, promises that if we spend time on the disciplines we will learn to fly, so to speak. We will change.

Similarly, Dallas Willard argues in *The Spirit of the Disciplines* that without rigorous training and practice we are like an athlete who comes physically unprepared for the game. He concludes that if we practice the "Christ disciplines" of solitude, silence, prayer, meditation, study, service and sacrifice, we can become like Christ and stay in constant fellowship with God.

Yet I also hear voices like those of Rob, Allison, and Brother Lawrence.

One afternoon, over lunch with Rob, I mentioned I was writing a book on spiritual practice. Rob's face tightened, his shoulders raised.

He proceeded to tell me that too many Christians emphasize a narrow set of practices, especially scripture study and devotions. "I'm trying to learn to hear God beyond and outside of text," he said. "Many Christians around the world hear God and it's not through reading the bible."

My breath quickened when he said this. Then a few weeks later, I had a phone conversation with my friend Alison. She told me that her pastor grilled her over her scripture study and prayer time, recommending that she get up at 4:00 a.m. or at least 5:00 a.m., to spend an hour on each practice. She said she pretty much had to fight to keep her eyes open the whole time and that these disciplines felt more like law than freedom in Christ. We laughed and discussed that maybe what she really needed was the spiritual discipline of sleep.

Finally, the Renaissance monk Brother Lawrence says this, "We search for stated ways and methods of learning how to love God, and to come at that love we disquiet our minds by I know not how many devices; we give ourselves a world of trouble and pursue a multitude of practices to attain a sense of the Presence of God."

So I find myself in a quandary when trying to set down the rules of the spiritual growth and health game. Should I practice 65 different disciplines? I don't think Calhoun expects this, and I don't have enough years left to spend adequate time on each. Should I focus on what Willard seems to think are the Jesus disciplines? Should I make up my own disciplines, based on my current life needs or perhaps in emulation of Christians around the world? Should I forget trying at all and just leave things to God?

---

3. And you?

In your journal, or during a small-group sharing time,
complete the thoughts:

"I think (don't think) spiritual practice is a biblical construct, because... "

"I've been taught that the most important spiritual practice is..."

"One spiritual practice that has always baffled me is ..."

"If I could decide my own 'program' of spiritual practice, it would look like... [be honest, not compliant, here]"

After a while, the mama and papa cardinals decide I'm about as dangerous as a giant acorn. They ignore me and set themselves to dealing with cardinal junior. Papa sits in the pine, silently watching—a forbidding guard should I decide to morph into a cat or some such threatening creature. Mama begins a conversation in word and gesture. She comes within a few feet of junior and chirps, "This way! This way!" The baby fumbles his way through the undergrowth and finds a slender sapling. Using his tiny feet, he inches his way up.

Then mama flies to his left, a little further off than the first time. "This way! This way!" she chirps. The baby flaps his wings and does a little hop to a nearby branch. Not an accomplished tight-rope walker yet, he wobbles a bit upon landing. I hold my breath. He doesn't fall.

I watch this game for about an hour. Mama on the left. Mama on the right. "This way! This way!" Junior hop, skip, flapping gradually higher and higher, sapling branch by sapling branch. Junior wobbling, almost falling, me holding my breath. I watch until he makes it to the camouflage of the leafy vine that has lassoed the pine. Then I go into the house and write about mama, papa and baby in my journal.

In the end, I decide to adopt the cardinals' rules. It seems to me that God is like the mama and papa birds. As Julian of Norwich has suggested, he made me, he loves me, he protects me. Furthermore, he leads me upward and onward, wheeling in close then moving off where I can't see him, but always calling "This way! This way!" Yet it's up to me to inch my way up, flap, hop, even wobble.

In this scenario, God is on the left. Then he's on the right. If there's any rule at all, it is *listen*. But the direction and the path can change (now it is an oak sapling to the right, then it is over to the maple that sways in the breeze). My job is not so much to practice a rigid set of disciplines as to pay attention.

On a practical level, this means that though I'll take time to read and learn about spiritual practices of various kinds, I decide not to be married to particular ones as The Only Path. Instead, I'll see what comes. This isn't the most comfortable way to conduct a flying lesson; once I realize how amorphous it seems, I feel a minor anxiety attack bubbling up. How will I ever learn to fly without an exact instruction manual?

I calm myself with wisdom from Wendell Berry and sincerely apologize for mixing a farming metaphor with my Lesson from the Birds. But here it is. "To live as a farmer, one has to come to the local watershed and the local ecosystem and deal well or poorly with them. One must encounter directly and feelingly the topography and the soils of one's particular farm, and treat them well or poorly." In other words, one must stand within the limits of one's plot and take stock. This also applies, I suggest, to anyone who seeks to work with the soul.

So it ends like this. Me and God, surveying the soil. Leaning down, rubbing the dirt between our fingers. Testing the density, the weight and scent. Tasting the balance of minerals. The rules of the farming-and-flying game will go like so: I'll continue in the program I've already understood, come outside alone every day for a year. I'm hoping this solitude will be a space in time that allows me to experience the beckoning of God... *Come to me.* I'll try to pay attention to what I hear, if anything. Maybe I'll practice some spiritual disciplines or simply receive them as a gift, as I spend time reading and learning more about them.

Now I wonder, is that the Holy Spirit, trilling somewhere beyond the vines, *I can revise your life. Look, I'm ready to pour out my spirit on you. I'm ready to tell you all I know.* Can I be sure? Does it matter? Flight begins: I take hold of my first slender sapling and inch my way towards his love.

Playing towards God & discovery

Transformation Math: Are there things in your life you wish God would sweep away? Difficult emotions? Habits that leave you feeling lesser as a person (or seem to leave others feeling lesser as persons)? What do you hope God might replace these with? Jot your ideas.

Now create math problems using your jottings, to demonstrate your prayers for transformation. They might look something like this: controlling – fear = release. Or, irritability – shouting = patience. Maybe you're more the geometry type. Could you take a quality like "detached" and draw two separate circles? Then, draw two overlapping circles as a prayer for connection? What would it take to get the circles overlapping? Add that to your equation. Play with different combinations of math problems and figures to demonstrate your desires for change.

Releasing Burdens: What might be holding you back from experiencing transformation? Maybe grief or fear, anger or mistrust. If you live in a place where you have outdoor access, take a strong bag with you and gather heavy rocks. Name them "grief," "fear," whatever, and put them in your bag. Walk for a while carrying your burden. When your arms are tired, set your burden down and empty your bag as an act of prayer, asking God to refill it with His light gifts of grace. If you don't have outdoor access, use large books and carry them around the house/apartment for a while until you are wishing for a lighter burden.

Your Life as a Garden: Maybe you need more patience or less fear. Perhaps you hope to develop greater generosity. What do you really want and need? Sketch your life as if it's a garden, then color it in. Give attention to the following concerns: What's the soil like? What's growing or struggling to grow? Are there any new plants you want to add? Where would you put them? You can label your drawing if you like.

Week 2 prayer

Father, Son and Holy Spirit, I admire your partnership and love. As I continue this journey of discovery, I ask you to teach me the mystery of how to live in a way that mirrors your divine life.

Sabbath on the page

At least several times this week (or every day if you can swing it), try resting on the page by engaging in stream-of-consciousness writing. Do this for at least several pages, and you might be pleasantly surprised to find a sense of peace. If you're like me, you fear that someone will read your uncensored thoughts. If necessary, write messy. Write so messy you can't even read your own writing.

Blog it, to process and share

It's the end of week two. Consider blogging about your experience. If you don't blog, you can do a "week-in-review" in your journal or write a letter to a friend or God. You could include:

- An idea that was new to you, or a quote you appreciated
- Something you liked about your experience
- Something you felt anxious or unsure about
- Any questions you have (no need to answer them; sometimes the asking is the most important step)
- Things you were reminded of: a story, memory, piece of art or music, bible verse or prayer, poem, current or historical event

Look: contemplation • week 3

Looking is the beginning of seeing.

— *Sister Corita Kent*

A tree is a tree. Roots, brown trunk, branches, green leaves or needles. Reaching, swaying, rustling. I can recognize a tree, sure as I can blink. All my life I've been walking beneath them, taking shade from them in summer, fire from them in winter. I know trees.

Bushes. I know bushes too. They dot the landscape, crowd the woods, punctuate flowerbeds in front yards. Bushes are also roots, brown branches, green leaves—bobbing under birds, sheltering spiders. (Really, bushes need to face the facts: they are just short, fat trees.)

This is pretty much what I thought, until I began to mark out a temple in the little woods.

Marking out a temple sounds vaguely sacrilegious, like I'm going to carve up a cadre of gods to put between pillars of pine and maple. My neighbors might not go for that sort of land use, but they needn't worry. "To mark out a temple" is just one meaning of the word *contemplation*.

Contemplation is an obvious choice of spiritual practice, as I come each day to a place where there's not much to do but drift in my thoughts. True, some monastics deemed contemplation to be more about control than drifting. In *The Cloud of Unknowing*, Ira Progroff says that "the Contemplative was a person who undertook, either within monastery or secular living, to control his thoughts or feelings by means of special disciplines in order to become capable of a closer relationship with God. Far from being passive... the contemplative life is decidedly active..."

But other voices also speak—voices that say things more suited to my ambiguous approach of sitting in the same spot every day, drinking tea and dozing beneath the trees. Gerald May points out, for instance, that contemplation "assumes an open, all-embracing, panoramic quality." Calhoun adds that contemplation involves gazing, with faith, hope and love, which can potentially increase our capacity for patience. These descriptions of contemplation sound like fancy ways to say *drift and doze*, albeit lovingly and spiritually. This will be my brand.

---

1. And you?

In your journal, or during a small-group sharing time,
complete the thoughts:

"I would define contemplation as... "
"Maybe I am contemplating when I 'mark out a temple' by..."
"I allow myself (do not allow myself) to drift and doze, by..."

What should I contemplate? This is a stickier question than one might assume.

Leonardo DaVinci was one of the greatest artists the world has ever seen. How did he come to be so? Surely there was innate talent, something in his brain that connected the dots of life and form more complexly than the next person. But there was also an openness to the world, an "all-embracing" quality to his observations, that worked in tandem with his raw abilities.

DaVinci once said, "Do not despise my opinion when I remind you that it should not be hard for you to stop sometimes and look into the stains of walls, or ashes or a fire, or clouds, or mud or like places, in which, if you consider them well, you may find really marvelous ideas...."

By indistinct things the mind is stimulated to new inventions."

I have no doubt that DaVinci would find my backyard experiment valuable.

Yet in my experience of Christendom, there's little room for the DaVinci approach to spirituality. I was taught to value the contemplation of Scripture above all. Forget about black-eyed Susans, psychedelic green bees, the dying dogwood. And who needs wall stains or, least of all, mud, to stimulate the mind and heart to growth?

Opinions about text superiority are sometimes expressed quite strongly. I remember a comment that showed up one day on my prayer and devotion blog, "Anytime we say 'Regular prayer and reading the Bible is not enough,' we insult Jesus..."

Have I gone completely off the map of acceptable spiritual practice, in coming outside with an openness to moth and monarch, white clover and catbird?

Maybe, but I consider the prophet Ezekiel. I used to think he was, well, unusual. Wheels within wheels, and such things. Until I began to contemplate the pine. One day, alternately gazing at the maples to the right and the pine overhead, it occurred to me that the two grow quite differently.

Maples have a Nile-River-delta thing going on—a trunk that divides and divides, river to stream to rivulets to sky. White Pine is wheels within wheels. The trunk is an axle flung straight to heaven and branches grow out from it like spokes. Each major branch pokes stiffly outward. Then again, the minor branches circle it like spokes. And so on. Wheels within wheels. Ezekiel tree.

Perhaps the prophet was a bit unusual to speak of wheels within wheels, or maybe he had seen a pine like mine, which gave him a visual language to describe what he saw and experienced spiritually.

So, is it an insult to Jesus to look for him not only in Scripture but also in the trees? Calvin Miller asserts, "Christ doesn't just lord it over the natural world. He inhabits it. This is not to cozy up to any Eastern views that Christ is one with the elements of his world, but Jesus is related to all life that he created. " In Miller's schema, it's possible for Ezekiel to be fully sane, to see God on the clouds, in the wheels, maybe even in the trees.

Rabbi Mike Comins further explores the relationship between God and creation, the question of text versus nature. Leaving synagogue one Rosh Hoshanah, he goes on a hike. Putting away his prayer shawl he glances from his prayer book to the sky. Says Comins, "I thought about the great debate that has occupied Jewish thinkers over the millennia....Where do we find God? From where does revelation come? Wilderness or the Book? Nature or Torah?"

He concludes we can find God in both, especially since Torah was granted in wilderness.

Which is to say that Ezekiel may have been onto something when he translated his vision of wheels-within-wheels into words. And maybe, just maybe I am on to something too, waiting for the wind to speak, turn my days into paragraphs and pages.

---

2. And you?

In your journal, or during a small-group sharing time,
complete the thoughts:

"When I put spiritual experiences into words, I draw on other experiences such as..."
"Words communicate differently than nature, because..."
"Nature communicates things that words cannot, such as..."

It took me a while to develop respect for the bushes—to notice how some grow in the pattern of intricate lace, and others put forth leaves that, in their early stages, look like fleur-de-lis. I discovered, with time, that the thorn bush was ridged. Dark amber stalks stood brittle. And the wood-winged bushes indeed have wings, or maybe propellers, or paddles, which make them look like an elongated windmill wheel.

When I found my proper respect for the bushes, I honored them in poetry. It'd been a hard day. I hadn't been patient, the way the practice of contemplation promises I can be. Anyhow, on that day I gave the bushes a heart of wisdom over and above the trees.

"Matriarch"

Children off to bed, chatter secrets.
I descend red oak stairs, reach for downy coat,
walk out beneath the moon.

Sled in hand, I pick my way to secret place,
settle plastic red, breathe deep to unwind tight-sprung
day, lie down and look towards the pine.

Branched arms are softness, feathered cradle
calling. Trunk is hips, come to say, sit;
gone is the needle-sharp talk of day.

Nearby, grandmother-curved bush looks
to lap in silence, remembers how it was with young ones,
remembers how grace used to drift in with the night.

If the way to contemplation comes "not through effort but through darkness" as Gerald Sittser says, if grace can drift in with the night, I might be in luck. I've come to this outdoor place feeling emotionally dark. I bring a childhood past that's also somewhat dark. In other words, I bring a shadowy inner landscape that may be crucial to the contemplation process.

In some ways, it seems too self-focused to let the inner landscape be part of our reaching towards the Divine. Spiritual practice is supposed to be about God, isn't it? Yet if the word *contemplative* also means "putting together," which it does, then it may be needful to search the darkness, the broken pieces of life, with an openness that these are somehow important parts of communion with God.

Parker Palmer says we need the grounding of psychology to keep contemplative insight from becoming "untethered, floating above the realities of our embodied lives." I have a personal psychology: child of divorce multiple times, first at age three; child of alcoholism—particularly that of my grandfather and stepfather. What does this really mean? What does it mean, for instance, that a small child experiences divorce as a "sudden death" which creates an "overwhelming internal panic" and that alcoholics can't give us what we need in terms of love, emotional security and approval? How will I contemplate these questions? Maybe I'll simply bring them with me, an offering to God, set aflame in my makeshift temple. Will DaVinci be proved right? Might I find something vital in ashes or a fire?

---

3. And you?

In your journal, or during a small-group sharing time,
complete the thoughts:

"If the way to contemplation comes through darkness, I..."

"I think my inner landscape is (is not) crucial to contemplation, because..."

"My personal psychology includes..."

Playing towards God & discovery

Live It Openly: If you have access to a natural space, go outside this week, every day, rain or shine, bitter cold or unbearable heat. Bring a tarp or blanket and lie down for at least 15 minutes, but preferably up to an hour. You're not here to make something happen. You're here to participate simply by sensing the world. Allow yourself to drift. If something interests you, follow it lightly. Maybe you feel a leaf between your fingers, maybe you gaze at the pearl gray insect that lands on your arm. Perhaps you catch a scent on the breeze or hear a bird you've never heard before. Maybe not. There is no agenda.

As May explains, contemplation is "centeredness in the present moment. This is the 'timeless moment' of the mystics, the 'eternal now'— what the twentieth-century educator Thomas Kelly called 'continuously renewed immediacy.'" So let yourself go, the way the Psalmist David probably did all those days and nights in the fields... and in so doing, heard the murmurs of God. If you live in an urban area, you can still go outside. Lie down on a bench or sit against a tree in the park. Can you hear God's whispers, even in the bustle of the city square?

Unstring: Picture certain issues/emotions/elements of your personal psychology to be like a cord that binds you. Can you feel them cutting in? Do you wish the ties could be loosened? As a kind of prayer, invite the Spirit to begin unwinding the invisible cords; to feel the hope of this, act out the unwinding with your body. If you prefer, draw a picture of yourself and what binds you, then draw a series of pictures that illustrate the ties coming undone.

Week 3 prayer

God of the Universe, Maker of heaven and earth, how can I find you? Let me be open to your voice wherever it speaks, to your hand wherever it touches, to your fragrance wherever it drifts on the wind.

Sabbath on the page

At least several times this week (or every day if you can swing it), try resting on the page by engaging in stream-of-consciousness writing. Do this for at least several pages. It is another form of "drifting and dozing" that may lead you into contemplative openness.

Blog it, to process and share

It's the end of week three. Consider blogging about your experience (if you don't want to blog, you can do a "week-in-review" in your journal or write a letter to a friend or God). You could include:

- An idea that was new to you, or a quote you appreciated
- Something you liked about your experience
- Something you felt anxious or unsure about
- Any questions you have (no need to answer them; sometimes the ask-

ing is the most important step)

• Things you were reminded of: a story, memory, piece of art or music, bible verse or prayer, poem, current or historical event

Weep: celebration • week 4

We spend... too little time experiencing
the griefs themselves. The result is that these griefs
remain hidden and never open us to our joys.

— *David Whyte*

The house gapes at me from the far side of the lawn, its aluminum storm windows reflecting an air of doubt and boredom. Must I explain myself to a 1930's Tudor? Okay, this is my story. I am in a makeshift temple in my back yard: a rusty chain link fence separates my property from the neighbors' on three sides; I always sit in the ivy under the white pine, never in the grass.

English ivy is the boisterous type. Anything that lives through winter pert and green must necessarily be energetic, so of course it defies delineation. If I didn't take the lawnmower to it with some determination, it would sneak down the hill, climb up tan stucco, wind its way over handles and windows, eat the house maybe (which, on the bright side, would save me from having to explain myself). So I dutifully mow the ivy bald, leaving wistful vines.

The chain link fence has been here so long it is sunken, rusted. But, it's going nowhere. Even the squirrels know this, and they've permanently incorporated it into their metro line. Like the squirrels, I count on the fence. In spring I clean to its edges and rest sticks against it. It keeps the neighbor children, who like to throw large yellow Tonka trucks at the cedar next door, from using me for target practice.

Then there's the pine. She's a thin barrier between the sky and my daily resting place. Flexible and prone to seasons, she is one day bronzed, another day slicked with ice, still another moment blued with the sky's reflection. Sometimes rain drips past her arms, or snow. I am mildly vulnerable to what the sky sends down.

1. And you?

In your journal, or during a small-group sharing time,
complete the thoughts:

"If I were to choose a 'temple' right now [a place where I could spend
time in discovery], it would be [describe it in detail, whatever it is]..."
"The protective aspects of my 'temple' are..."
"The adventurous aspects of my 'temple' are..."

Celebration does not occur in a vacuum. The Jewish people know this,
so long is their history of commanded festivals. Rather, celebration takes
place in containers of various forms, temples in time and space, with
particular shapes and boundaries. There is a predictability and holistic
nature to this kind of celebration that is absent in some Christian sug-
gestions to practice celebration simply by doing what makes us feel joyful.

Calhoun suggests choosing a context, and in this way we begin to approach the more traditional understanding of celebration. Powerful celebrations, after all, happen in predictable contexts. Take the Jewish
festival of Sukkot, the Festival of Booths. To celebrate Sukkot, families
construct a temporary structure, semi-open to the sky, in which they
practice acts of remembrance, eat special foods, and entertain strangers.
Likewise, the Jewish Passover celebration recreates a similar context year
after year, even if it takes place in different settings, by including a
predictable set of readings, symbols, rituals and events.

One wonders if all this predictability is too static, like a temple built
simply from a chain link fence with no unruly ivy and no ceiling cracks

through which the sky could leak. Yet on Sukkot, the dwelling-place open to the sky must offer no little adventure on a rainy night. And during Passover, the order of events includes space for both fence and ivy, tradition and creative personal interpretation.

As a child of both divorce and alcoholism, I have frailties on both sides of the celebration question: *structure* and *joyful freedom*.

It's no secret that both divorce and alcoholism can create chaos, where the basic predictability is *unpredictability*, where the prevailing structure is *disorganization*. I was a small child when my parents divorced, and small children psychologically experience the breakup as a "sudden death" of one or both parents. Wallerstein calls divorce a watershed experience that permanently alters a child's life, as it introduces a sense of danger regarding relationships. She concludes that the resulting anxiety "represents the end of childhood."

Along with the end of childhood comes the end of remembrance, another form of structure. Children retain little sense of their family history, including everything from their parents' courtship to memories of holidays and vacations. Wallerstein notes, "the parents' interaction was a black hole—as if the couple had vanished from memory and the children's conscious life."

This holds true for me. The single memory I have of my parents together is an incident in the kitchen, when my father threw a mop, shouted, walked out and slammed the door. When that door shut, something inside me shut with it. Memory became a sieve, mourning a companion. It's not like I really knew this about myself. But then the sky leaked a gift.

---

2. And you?

In your journal, or during a small-group sharing time,

complete the thoughts:

"My favorite celebration is..."
"The central elements of the celebration seem to be..."
"The emotions that the central elements of the celebration evoke are..."

I always found it puzzling that my aunt called me an "old soul." And my mother tells me people used to say I was like a little old lady. Since then, I've been called "serious" and "intense," but none of these things ever rang true. Wasn't I a pretty light-hearted person?

Yet, looking back at journals from my time outdoors, I see entry after entry that says things like... "I feel so incredibly sad. A deep sadness that I literally feel in my body, a coolness, a quaver." Or this, "I come again in sorrow, weighted with unknown griefs."

At first I saw this new consciousness of grief as a negative thing. It hurt so badly. Never in my life had I experienced anything that came so close to chronic depression. I began to worry. Could I escape it? Should I try? What if grief had something important to tell me?

David Whyte says we spend too little time experiencing griefs, so they stay hidden, and our joy stays hidden with them. "It is as if the two are simply two ends of the same whole. Remove the experience at one end of the scale by curtailing our capacity for grief and the whole emotional body shrinks to a bland middle, curtailing equally our capacity for joy."

Shrunken to a bland middle. Before grief's stubborn arrival, didn't this describe my emotional landscape and the shape of my capacity to celebrate? Maybe anxiety over my parent's divorce had long ago done that to me. Also, as Beattie notes, people who live with alcoholics often refuse to enjoy life. Fine. I couldn't take that away, but perhaps I needed to backtrack into grief.

I think about how some Jews sit shiva for a week after a death. During this time, the bereaved stays cocooned in the house, not washing, not looking in mirrors, not doing much of anything but feeling the pain and experiencing the full measure of grief. This is followed by carefully staged rituals of re-entry into society, at special intervals, to scaffold the process of mourning and healing as much as possible.

So I began to wade into grief by talking to myself. "You grew up in the chaos and disappointment of an alcoholic household." "In a way, you lost both mother and father at the age of three." (I was reading literature on divorce and discovering that mother disappears as much as exited father, since she collapses emotionally and becomes unable to reach out to her children.) "You are still a child wishing your parents' marriage would miraculously come back to life, even though you consciously understand that's ridiculous."

Months later, still apparently grieving, I wrote this poem and cried my way through it. It's called "Father" but it speaks to the sorrow of losing mother and father as a couple...

"Father"

I used to think you'd
ride back into our lives,
dismount red convertible Pontiac,
stride into the kitchen
past grey splintered barn, dead-end road,
burning barrel, wind-whipped clothesline,
pick up the mop you'd thrown across
our black and white checkered floor,
put it back near hanging iron sink,
kiss mother on the cheek and play
fly-like-a-birdie with me again.

What happens when we experience such traumas as children? Whyte notes we can "unconsciously refuse to grow any older" in the part of us that's been traumatized "until that trauma is resolved." Oddly, this seems to be paired with a false kind of maturity, an old-soulness like I mentioned before. Whyte calls it a *callous*, a wound carefully isolated, in need of opening and resolution.

Can we really resolve the trauma of what's-done-is-done? The breakup of a family years ago? The years of chaos in an alcoholic household? I'm doubtful about the possibility of healing. But I consider that holistic celebration offers a chance for us to grow up emotionally and spiritually, because it gives back what situations like divorce and alcoholism steal: remembrance of grief, gifts of joy, opportunities for structure and freedom.

My kids' favorite religious holiday isn't Christian, it's Jewish: Passover. Maybe they instinctively understand the fullness of a holiday that begins with remembrance of grief, bestows joy through food shared with family, offers the structure of tradition as well as the freedom of play (how they love to do an impromptu retelling of the Exodus with finger puppets!)

Coming outdoors, I began to celebrate more holistically. There was structure; every day I came out, hot drink and little book of Psalms in hand. There was freedom; sometimes I came while morning mist still hung, other times on starry nights. Grief asked me to make room for it on the sled. I scootched over and it came.

Would it make any difference? I wasn't sure.

---

3. And you?

In your journal, or during a small-group sharing time, complete the thoughts:

"If I had to pinpoint a painful time in my life, it might be..."

"If I could say anything to myself about my painful time, I'd say..."

"Religious celebration and healing of painful times seem (do not seem) connected, because..."

Playing towards God & discovery

It is good to take grief and give it a place in our celebrations, alongside joy. Gertrude Nelson, author of *To Dance with God* notes that such ritual-making can help us deal with the important phases and experiences of our lives, because we make conscious what is otherwise unconscious and prone to getting stuck in neurotic structures and habits.

Too often, our lives have been arranged the other way around. As Nelson reminds, "... we are overawed by our ritual habits, our fears and symptoms. In place of the periodic holy fast, we have become slaves to our perennial diets. In exchange for 'carrying our cross' in the constructive suffering that every life requires, we complain of low back pain. The old taboos, which we think we are freed of, crop up as new varieties of superstitions, and we take another vitamin."

The solution is to take seriously the power of symbols, rhythm and ritual. Liturgy and church calendars offer possibilities. But we're also free to borrow and create. In my home, for instance, we've adapted some of the elements of the Jewish Sukkot festival to flesh out our family Christmas Eve tradition. These kinds of practices are often large enough to encircle whatever life has brought our way. We might also want to intentionally go deeper, regarding our specific needs and dreams.

A Circle of Ritual: Think about what you've discovered so far in your explorations. Are there things you need to grieve or celebrate? Areas you wish to change or strengthen? Cut some circles and label them with these hopes. If you like, arrange them in your journal, also in a circle. What might you put in the middle? On the outside?

Consider what kinds of rituals you might engage in to bring healing or blessing to the needs/dreams you wrote on your circles. For example, if you labeled one circle "despair," you might decide to engage in a ritual of hope each morning. Maybe you could write out your sorrows, roll them up and put them in a large bottle, reminding yourself that God collects our tears and holds them close to his heart (Ps. 56:8). Maybe then you could light a candle and whisper a thought of praise.

If we choose to create our own celebrations, here are some basic elements Nelson suggests we include: sound (stories, readings, music, cries, silence), gestures (procession, dance, clapping, harvesting, planting, burials), natural elements (seeds, rocks, oil, fruit, branches, flowers, herbs, water, fire, wind... which is harnessed by other elements like flags, streamers, banners), handmade items, and food. Nelson's book is also a good source for becoming familiar with the Christian liturgical calendar. In addition, I've enjoyed borrowing from our Jewish roots, using *Celebration: The Jewish Book of Festivals*.

Week 4 prayer

Lord of Celebration, who turned water into wine for joy, who drank wine in sorrow at the Last Supper, teach me to celebrate as you did, as you do.

Sabbath on the page

At least several times this week (or every day if you can swing it), try resting on the page by engaging in stream-of-consciousness writing. Do this for at least several pages. It can be a form of drawing a circle around a moment, of creating a "makeshift temple." Don't be surprised if you come to value the safety and adventure of this promised place of discovery.

Blog it, to process and share

It's the end of week four. Consider blogging about your experience. If you don't blog, you can do a "week-in-review" in your journal or write a letter to a friend or God. You could include:

• An idea that was new to you, or a quote you appreciated
• Something you liked about your experience
• Something you felt anxious or unsure about
• Any questions you have (no need to answer them; sometimes the asking is the most important step)
• Things you were reminded of: a story, memory, piece of art or music, bible verse or prayer, poem, current or historical event

Sky: gratitude • week 5

Between the time a gift comes to us
and the time we pass it along,
we suffer gratitude.

— Lewis Hyde

The ceiling of my makeshift temple is vast and changeable. One morning it is pearls, strung between the wider universe and me. Another moment it is pink seashells on ocean foam. At night it might be cobalt glass I could fall into, never come home. Sometimes, beyond reasoning, the midnight sky is a peach that says, "Bite."

It is not unusual for various gifts to dart, plummet, drift or drip from this changeable space. I open my eyes and see dark grey birds, like fighter pilots careening. I close my eyes and feel the unexpected "tip, tip" of fine rain pricking my cheeks. Seeds in white silk coats try to plant themselves on my arms. Pine needles use my teacup as a heliport.

The sky is also a sponge that sucks up offerings. Steam from my mug rises and dissipates. Mourning doves chirrup and disappear past rooflines. Clouds hurry on wind, kiss and follow currents towards towns more amenable to celestial passion. When the sky is feeling ravenous, shingles fly off the roof, tumble past the grey-blue house.

~

Gertrud Nelson observes that, through the ages, religious architecture made allowance for the sky, understanding it as either the literal or symbolic dwelling place of the Divine. Accordingly, the Roman Pantheon had a hole in its roof, to allow comings and goings of gods, that they might connect with the human spirit. Early Pentecost rites utilized holes in the ceiling to drop burning straw down to the faithful and allow the possible escape of a white dove released in the room. Baroque believers had to settle for a symbolic opening, a circle of sky painted on the ceiling, displaying the tread of God and angels.

Nelson concludes that just as religious architecture made allowance for spiritual exchange, so we make room in our lives, through custom and ceremony, "a holy space, set aside, that also works as a shelter. But while we must shore up and make firm our container on all sides, our remaining 'open to the Spirit' means allowing some opportunity for the spontaneous and unexpected to enter. We... leave openings."

---

1. And you?

In your journal, or during a small-group sharing time, complete the thoughts:

"If I were to pinpoint a 'holy space' in my life it would/could be..."
"The idea of a holy space interests (bothers) me, because..."
"I'm comforted by (afraid of) the idea of leaving openings, because..."

I heard it through a friend. Someone had said of me, "She seems closed in her spirit." This was news. I always considered myself to be a fairly open person, thankful for life and its gifts. Still, this seemed to coincide with the cautious observation of another friend, "You're kind of detached." These images of being closed off, isolated, seemed otherworldly. Wasn't I always the first to say thank you in a social situation? Didn't I have a deep desire to be connected to others? Hadn't I felt, with a sense of gratitude, that God had brought me thus far, miraculously so?

Maybe. But it appeared that the gratitude I thought was mine either didn't exist or wasn't making it through to the outside. At least to certain people.

Adele Calhoun says the practice of gratitude can free us and help us be aware of the abundance of gifts in our lives. It can also, she notes, help us treasure the people around us. So I gave it my best shot. The practice mostly involved positive thinking and positive saying. List good things in a gratitude journal. Say "thank you" to God. Say "thank you" to others. Try not to make comparisons between your own situation and that of others. Give presents. Sing. Spend time with friends. All of it looked suspiciously like what I'd done most of my life.

Yet the practice seemed powerless to change my inner landscape. Somebody who has the athlete-view of spiritual life is going to question my lack of discipline and tell me if only I had tried a little harder, penned more lists, spent more time, I would have been made ready for the game. I want to say, "Let's talk about the sky."

As the writer of an online poetry column, I enjoy providing writing prompts. People seem to like the challenge of composing with a bit of direction. Once I offered the line "if memories were sparrows" and an anonymous blogger left this poem in my comment box...

If memories
were sparrows, spiked
tails flashing black
across the sky

Be
Or mourning doves
red velvet down
upon the snow

Still

Remember how
the birds were eaten
by the sky

Be

And then alone
after the melted snow
lay down

Still

The poem has some wonderful nuances, but here's the part that stunned me with its simplicity and power, "Remember how/the birds were eaten/by the sky." The sky, vast and changeable, sometimes beautiful, is not seen as trustworthy. Any sparrow with its wits about it might consider staying grounded.

It occurred to me one day that I was like an earth-bound sparrow. I did not trust the sky. Growing up in an alcoholic household will do that to a person. The sky, or in other words, the social setting which is larger than us and that we look to for direction, the way we eventually learn to look to the Divine, does not invite exchange.

Instead, oppressive rules quell the open expression of feeling and the direct discussion of problems, personal and interpersonal. Combine this with the landscape of divorce, where a child learns to step lightly, put on a good face, keep secrets to protect Mom from Dad and vice versa, and you can end up with a person remarkably like me. I have a lot of well-worn nails, sturdy hammers, sheetrock, spackle and so forth that I use to patch up ceiling holes. The sky is safely shut out. I stay dry on the inside and the rain runs off the roof. And therein lies the problem. I stay dry on the inside. Likewise, any doves that might want to escape my boundaries and bless the world can get trapped. The house appears tidy, but it is immune to comings and goings, closed to the receiving and giving which is characteristic of gratitude.

---

2. And you?

In your journal, or during a small-group sharing time, complete the thoughts:

"I am (am not) a person of gratitude, as exhibited by..."
"When it comes to the 'sky', or authority structures, I tend to trust (not trust) them, because..."
"I feel comfortable (uncomfortable) expressing my feelings and problems openly, because..."

I have often heard spiritual practice described as serious discipline. In this scenario, we deny ourselves, put to death parts of our soul, or otherwise seek to coerce and control our spirits in an effort to grow. The underlying belief is that suffering will whip us into shape. This stems, partly perhaps, from a view of God that is authoritarian.

To this, I remember once sharing an image that had appeared in my mind, of a stone that spontaneously sprouted a wildflower. I marveled that this signaled impossible hope and God's generosity, to which I tentatively responded in gratitude. But one person immediately responded, "Maybe God has to smash you to heal you." I suppose that could be true at times—a kind of potter-clay or suffering-servant motif— but as a dominant perspective I find it to be along the lines of "remember how the birds were eaten by the sky." Threatening. Certainly not inviting for those of us who grew up already afraid of that which was bigger than we were, which proved itself dangerous and cannibalistic.

I wish I had a formula for promoting trust between a person and the sky—a kind of one-two-three for soul growth. The best I can say is *start small*. A person needn't run out into the open and invite lightning to strike. It's okay to do what the Jewish people do when they make their sukkah (temporary dwelling) for the festival of Sukkot. The dwelling is constructed open to the heavens, but it hedges a bit, allowing placement of slats or branches, foliage across the top of the structure. This creates a buffer, the way Nelson discusses how a few children she saw at the seashore created a buffer between themselves and the scary waves.

These children did not have the wherewithal to jump straight into the ocean, vast and powerful as it is. In fact, they barely wanted to stick their toes in the water. So they stayed in the sand and dug a hole, a potential water container on a much smaller scale. In time, they saw fit to begin coming and going to the larger body of water, carrying back a bucket at a time to fill their mini-ocean. Says Nelson, "In endless space, we create a fixed point to orient ourselves: a sacred space.... What is too vast and shapeless, we deal with in smaller, manageable pieces.... we turn our backs on what is too much and slowly create the form that will contain something of the uncontainable. In faith, we make such ritual and are grateful for the discipline that form lends." Form then, not discipline per se, becomes the buffer and the eventual conduit between the individual and the Divine, between the child and the ocean, between you and me and the sky.

---

3. And you?

In your journal, or during a small-group sharing time, complete the thoughts:

"Spiritual practice seems like serious discipline (play) to me, because..."
"I have been trained to think that growth happens through suffering more than (less than) play. I think this is based on... "
"One small thing that could promote more trust between me and God, or me and life in general, might be..."

Over time, in my makeshift temple, form began to have its way. I enjoyed the predictability of coming to my sacred space and remember one night in particular when it began to snow. I went out into the dark and settled myself beneath the white pine. It gave semi-shelter. Branches caught snowflakes, but also conspired with the sky, letting a few sparkly gifts drift down. Snow gathered lightly on my face, then began to melt and trickle down my cheeks. I opened my mouth and rivulets flowed in like a kind of holy drink. I felt the urge to laugh, to pray.

Was this some kind of beginning?

Playing towards God & discovery

Spiritual exchange, a rhythm of give-and-take with God and others, that is both based on and produces gratitude is not something we can easily practice. At least in my life, making lists of what I'm thankful for doesn't necessarily create the requisite openness and trust. These attributes require deeper soul work, of the kind we've been exploring.

As Lewis Hyde notes, gratitude is based on the receiving of transformative gifts. He says, "... with gifts that are agents of change, it is only when the gift has worked in us, only when we have come up to its level, as it were, that we can give it away again." In order to receive soul-alter-ing gifts, we must be open; we must also be open to pass them along.

Open 'n Close: For a week, every time you voice a complaint, make a mental note and jot it in your journal as soon as you can. Complaints are generally viewed as evidence that we are ungrateful people. And we may be. But complaints are also a window into our soul's fears and places of mistrust. While they can function as a barrier, keeping us closed to what we need from God and others, or even from ourselves, we can also learn something from them.

Using blocks or other items, build the *House of You* (or simply draw if you prefer). Leave openings as you build: doors, windows, a chimney. When you are finished, block the openings by taping your complaints over them. Do you see any patterns to your complaints? What do you make of them? Would you like to be able to remove them? What gifts might come inside if you did, and what gifts might leave you to bless the surrounding landscape? It's okay if you don't know the answers to these questions yet. Just sit with your discoveries.

Week 5 prayer

God of good gifts, please open me, to give and receive in gratitude, by helping me face my fears and struggles. Deepen my trust in you.

Sabbath on the page

At least several times this week (or every day if you can swing it), try resting on the page by engaging in stream-of-consciousness writing. Do this for at least several pages. Let your mind turn to things that make you afraid, jealous, or irritable, because they are strange keys to eventual gratitude. Be honest, not nice. It will take you further.

Blog it, to process and share

It's the end of week five. Consider blogging about your experience. If you don't blog, you can do a "week-in-review" in your journal or write a letter to a friend or God. You could include:

• An idea that was new to you, or a quote you appreciated
• Something you liked about your experience
• Something you felt anxious or unsure about
• Any questions you have (no need to answer them; sometimes the asking is the most important step)
• Things you were reminded of: a story, memory, piece of art or music, bible verse or prayer, poem, current or historical event

Open: prayer • week 6

See? This is who I am.

— *Gerald May, to God*

When I come outside, I generally settle in the same spot. Ground-cover is flattened into round evidence: somebody sits here every day. My nearest companions are a scraggly bush I call "grandmother bush," a slender oak sapling, arched forsythia and a single thorn bush. The presence of the white pine goes without saying.

These companions and their residents have taught me a thing or two. Now I understand why somebody coined "birds and the bees." Nature is... what shall I say? Unabashed.

This boldness often intrigued me. When the pine put out yellow fronds, pollen-dusted, I made pine needle tea and included them. (Pine bark is poisonous, but the needles and pollen make a nice medicinal brew.) Forsythia, it turns out, are also edible. So I topped my omelettes or granola with their flirty yellow skirts.

Still, my mother's voice cautioned from childhood days, "Don't eat anything wild. It might be poisonous." It should be no surprise, then, that I felt a twinge of guilt and fear when the thorn bush called.

A thorn flower looks like Lily of the Valley but more old-fashioned, dressed in lemon-ivory with a lace hem. From the center rises tiny orange guards and a green tongue with the barest hint of minute hairs and a pinhole of acceptance; liquid pearl trembles at the bulbous tip. When the pearl caught my attention, I plucked a quad of thorn flowers, turned them in morning light. Would this innocent flower make me sick? I briefly thought about Socrates and the wild hemlock plant (now that had a very sorry ending). I also seemed to remember something about Lily of the Valley being poisonous. Then I closed my eyes and touched the thorn's liquid pearl with my tongue.

Ah yes. Barely-there sugar: the thorn bush's invitation to sex.

---

1. And you?

In your journal, or during a small-group sharing time,
complete the thoughts:

"I am intrigued (nervous) about framing spiritual disciplines in the
language of art, grace or sex, because..."
"I feel like (don't feel like) I understand how to pray, because..."
"If prayer had a goal, it might be..."

Thinking about the spiritual disciplines, I struggle to describe their dynamics. Not long ago I went to a conference where the speaker used a tried-and-true analogy. Practice your scales and you'll be ready for the concert. Later, I had a conversation with a conference participant. The idea had resonated with him, as did the analogy of practicing the disciplines as a way to pass tests, win the game or secure victory in battle.

These analogies have their place (in fact, I've written about prayer's role in spiritual battle). Still, I'm ready to hear something different on the matter. Maybe, just maybe, spiritual disciplines could be cast in language that allows for more art, grace, and... well, really good sex. Particularly when it comes to the matter of prayer.

When I began thinking about prayer more consciously, about practicing it for some hoped-for goal, this is what I wrote in my journal: "I want to step more deeply into God and open my arms to others so I can take them more seriously." That's a good goal. What I hadn't considered was my own life makeup.

As counselor Murphy Toerner notes, family dysfunction teaches us things (denial of needs, feelings and thoughts; silence; perfectionism; keeping secrets) that may be opposed to these kinds of goals. We survive, she says by learning to "X" ourselves out as people.

Was I an X-woman? Perhaps. That might explain even silly situations like the night I hid a Snickers bar in the fridge and claimed, when asked, not to know about any resident chocolate. Wouldn't a person with a healthier sense of self just say, "Yeah, I've got a bar of chocolate, but I was saving it for myself"?

Compare me-and-my-Snickers to the woman in *Song of Songs*. Even with talk about her brothers mistreating her, I suspect she comes from a fairly functional family. I say this because she's a terrific thorn flower, broadcasting lace and sweetness to her Lover without fear, telling him just what she needs to get by.

When people take the allegorical view of *Song of Songs*, they paint the woman as Israel or the Church, and God as the Lover. I'll go with that interpretation in a minute. But I'd also like to suggest that the woman could be God. This isn't some pet theory about God as goddess. I'm simply making an observation based on my year in the woods; God can be fairly alluring in the same come-hither way, and we can be rather callous or dim about our approach, much like the *Song of Songs* Lover when he thrusts his hand through the latch. But I'm getting ahead of myself.

---

2. And you?

In your journal, or during a small-group sharing time, complete the thoughts:

"If I had to describe my 'life makeup', it might sound like..."

"My 'life makeup' seems to make me more ready (less ready) for prayer, because..."

"The thought of coming unprotected to God, as if to a Lover or Beloved, makes me feel..."

Sister Wendy Beckett, nun and art critic, says this about Piero Della Francesca's painting *The Baptism of Christ*, "Jesus is totally folded in on Himself, aware only of the Father and the Father's love, and its significance. This is what we long to be in prayer: one who is utterly given, stretching out beyond the immediate to the absolute reality of God." Similarly, she says, "The essential act of prayer is to stand unprotected before God. What will God do? He will take possession of us." Beckett, nun though she is, speaks the language of sex. *Utterly given. Stretching out. Unprotected.*

The Song of Songs woman uses similar language of extension and openness. She says, "Come, my beloved, let us go forth into the fields... let us go out early to the vineyards, and see whether the vines have budded, whether the grape blossoms have opened and the pomegranates are in bloom. There I will give you my love. The mandrakes give forth fragrance..." (Song of Songs, 7:11-13). Like the tiny ivory bells of my thorn bush, she invites entry, touch, breathing-deep. To pray like Beckett suggests, we must speak the woman's language, offer our bodies and souls to God in trust and passionate hope.

But there's more. We need to want the naked God too, the one whose fingers drip frankincense, myrrh and aloe. Song of Songs 4:11-15 says this of the woman, and do we hear the possibility of God, of Christ, in her aspect? "Your lips distill nectar... honey and milk are under your tongue [in you are] all trees of frankincense, myrrh and aloes... a garden fountain, a well of living water."

In 5:2, the woman is further described as "my dove, my perfect one." God language. Within the same passage, the Lover (can we imagine this as ourselves?) thrusts his hand through the latch opening. The Hebrew is full of double meanings suggesting a crude lovemaking that hasn't extended tenderness or asked, "Darling, beautiful one, what can I do for you?" After the Lover's cross approach and exit, the woman goes out seeking, calling. One thinks of Lady Wisdom, a Christ type, calling in the square. And what happens? Says the woman, "... the sentinels found me; they beat me, they wounded me, they took away my mantle." Still, she says, "If you find my beloved, tell him this: I am faint with love" (Song of Songs 5:6-8). Such language, oddly, takes me to the cross.

If for a moment we could see ourselves as the woman, if in the next moment, we could see God as the woman, how tender a picture of prayer we might paint—prayer as a place we come unprotected but also desiring God.

~

It's always informative to go to an online bookstore when researching a topic. So I went. I found a variety of items sure to boost any prayer life. Stuffed rabbits, bears, lambs and frogs promised to be cuddly and plush, and I could squeeze their tummies to say a classic prayer. (The lamb seemed appropro.) If I was afraid of the dark, I could order the "friendly little light, day or night, with its happily spinning shade." Besides creating light, motion, and magic, it comes with a prayer printed on its side. I thought it might function like a roulette wheel, whirling my requests heavenward; with any luck, I might get some answers. There were prayer flags, beads, even a cigarette case that said "Pray for beer." In the end, there was no product that would make me vulnerable and open to God. There was nothing to help me see God as my alluring Beloved. I left the Internet empty-handed.

Without a plush lamb to depend on, without a flag to wave in God's direction, I was back at the door latch needing to figure out how to do this prayer thing. The dictionary did nothing to console me, since the root of prayer is from the same Latin root that provides our word *precarious*, which means "uncertain, dependent on the will of another, risky." Like sex. After all, one can't assume a formula will bring good results—insert Tab A into Slot B for Result C; music, plus candles, plus bed equals ecstasy... no, it's more precarious than that, and so, it seems to me, is prayer.

---

3. And you?

In your journal, or during a small-group sharing time,
complete the thoughts:

"The words in Song of Songs that mirror words used of Christ are..."
"The trauma events in Song of Songs that mirror the trauma events in Christ's life are..."
"Formula prayer seems helpful (not helpful) in opening me to God; for instance..."

I'd like to think my personal struggles could be disentangled from my spirituality—that my inability to speak of needs or exchange myself in openness would only exist in my human relationships. Wouldn't it be nice if things were automatically different with God? Wouldn't it be great if I could bring my formulas, plush prayer lamb, flag, night light, and unhitch the God-door without having to get real and vulnerable?

For a long time I thought this was how things worked. But my time outdoors began to open me to myself, uncover grief and personal realities. I sat with discoveries from books about children of divorce and alcoholics and began to consider the person I became as a result of my childhood experiences.

I started to feel giddy with these new discoveries and desired a new sense of openness to God; maybe we could connect more deeply after all. I put some hope in this thought from Sister Wendy— God knows "exactly what we are, each of us, individually, what our genes are, what our upbringing has been" and "may well see [our] wordless, inchoate unhappiness as a form of prayer."

That was a real comfort, and for a few months this kind of prayer seemed to be making a difference. I began to feel a warmth and light in my spirit. Some days I would even talk aloud to God in the car, smile to the air.

Then the darkness came.

Playing towards God & discovery

Can we see "inchoate unhappiness" as a form of prayer? Or is our prayer too often a glossing over of the unhappy truth?

There is a place for lament. As Michael Card notes in *A Sacred Sorrow*, "Our failure to lament... cuts us off from each other. If you and I are to know one another in a deep way, we must not only share our hurts, anger and disappointments with each other... we must also lament them together before God who hears and is moved by our tears."

How can we practice lament? The power of online sharing as a form of corporate lament is sometimes underestimated, yet there are safe, inviting places to share the truth of our fears and hurts. *TheHighCalling.org* (my workplace) has become one of those arenas. For instance, one of our community members, Megan Willome, used lament-poetry to share what it was like to watch her mother struggle through cancer. Megan's words have often been a cherished offering to others; here is one poem she shared with the community...

"Still"

A clump of bluebonnets stands in the alley long past
Memorial Day. Usually they're fried by Easter.
In the spring they grow in green pastures, beside busy highways.
Now they look tired, out of place,
like they didn't get the notice that it's time
to make room for the warm wildflowers.
Tomorrow is Independence Day, and they're still there –
barely blue.
The Mexican Hats, the Wine Cups, even
the Firewheels have faded.
Those stubborn bluebonnets hang on like my mother
still thriving through cancer after cancer after cancer.

Compose Lament: Grieving and expression of hard truths is a highly personal act. Maybe music is your best language for lament. Or movement. Poetry or other forms of writing? Painting, collage, sculpture. Take some of the harder truths you've encountered about yourself so far in this course, and create a lament using one of these forms of communication. If you have a safe place to share it with others, consider doing so. Or simply offer it to God as a form of worship and prayer.

Richard Restak notes that our brains cannot keep more than one emotion in the foreground at a time; too much emphasis on depressive thoughts can send us into a depressive spiral. Isn't it interesting, then, that Psalms incorporate two elements into lament: the truth of our struggle, and the truth about God? It is not necessary to rush past your struggle (go ahead and sit with it for a few days), but you might plan a second lament stage by reshaping your words/movements/songs/pictures into the form of a Psalm (see below for a potential framework).

Put it in Psalm 118 (NRSV): Take your list of laments and insert them into this framework. You can use as many lament items as you like and at some point turn to observation of other kinds of things (sun, wind, rain, a child's touch, whatever). These are your "final items":

[1st lament item]
[Give thanks to the Lord for He is good, His love endures forever.]
[2nd lament item]
[Give thanks to the Lord for He is good, His love endures forever.]
[3rd lament item]
[Give thanks to the Lord for He is good, His love endures forever.]
[final items: move from lament to observation of something else]
[Give thanks to the Lord for He is good, His love endures forever.]

Week 6 prayer

Beloved God, you opened yourself to the world in Creation and at the Cross. I sense your great tenderness and beckoning. Sweet One, what can I do for you?

Sabbath on the page

At least several times this week (or every day if you can swing it), try resting on the page by engaging in stream-of-consciousness writing. Do this for at least several pages. Don't censor your sadness, confusion, questions, angers. Openness before God can create an unparalleled form of connection. See everything you write as a form of prayer, unformed and odd as it may be.

Blog it, to process and share

It's the end of week six. Consider blogging about your experience (if you don't want to blog, you can do a "week-in-review" in your journal or write a letter to a friend or God). You could include:

• An idea that was new to you, or a quote you appreciated
• Something you liked about your experience
• Something you felt anxious or unsure about
• Any questions you have (no need to answer them; sometimes the asking is the most important step)
• Things you were reminded of: a story, memory, piece of art or music, bible verse or prayer, poem, current or historical event

Gone: presence • week 7

... do that until you ache, until you ache,
then come to me again.

— *Rumi*

It is winter and a single berry hangs from the thorn bush, like a drop of blood suspended 'midst spikes and brittle arches. Against a backdrop of snow, the tiny fruit is startling. I can't deny its presence.

All summer, the yard had been pushing towards seed. Not only the thorn bush but also raspberries, blueberries, currants, grasses I neglected to mow, purple asters and dandelions. Pollen and stamen frolicked, only to be silenced when passion subsumed itself in dark cradles, hard-coated. Hidden energies drifted on the wind, were eaten, fell to the ground to sit motionless through winter.

By now, it is so cold I can see my breath, but I take off one black glove. Careful to skirt thorns, I touch the berry. It is firm, smooth, resolute. I do not pick or attempt to crush it. Let it hang, a drop of blood from a crown of thorns.

~

When I was a child I fantasized I'd be a nurse. Then I discovered I didn't like blood. My growing-up years did nothing to reverse my aversion. I remember hearing my stepmother Beasie talk about her "monthly"; I knew what she meant and could tell by the code words that this subject carried a measure of shame. My hunch was confirmed when as a teenager I sat in on an adult bible study one night, only to hear a graphic discussion about Isaiah 64's "filthy rags" passage; I considered sliding under the table, but instead sat motionless and blushing. As a grown woman reading Leviticus, I never found much comfort either. In its pages, menstruating women are deemed unclean and off-limits for sex.

But recently I've begun to find a different perspective.

It started at a conference where someone asked a question of Debbie Blue. She had just spoken about her book *Sensual Orthodoxy*, which is about the wild, living nature of scripture. A man in the audience asked her about Levitical laws on menstruation.

Blue smiled and asked if anyone might like to answer the question. As it happened, I had just been spending time in Leviticus, so I tentatively offered, "I'm thinking the book is largely an attempt at grace on the human, governance level, which means that laws on menstruation are also a form of grace."

This thought began to redeem my stance on blood and the idea of mandated separation.

---

1. And you?

In your journal, or during a small-group sharing time, complete the thoughts:

"When I think of blood, I think of..."
"To me, blood is a sign of joining (separation), because..."
"Separation might be a form of grace in situations such as..."

In reading about how alcoholism changes the non-alcoholic members of a family into "co-dependents," I was surprised to find myself so clearly described. Co-dependents are often unable to endure separation. In an attempt for security and acceptance, they tend towards *total involve-*

ment. With relationships, this can mean undue intensity and frequency of contact. With work, it can mean the same. We co-dependents are, at first glance, dream employees who will give all, perfect all, perform all. As friends, we initially seem perfect too; we try so hard, give so much, are endlessly available.

Really, co-dependents should be required to read Levitical laws on menstruation. Before they reach midlife and its potential crisis.

I used to think that mid-life crisis was a myth or some kind of excuse for becoming a 40-year-old teenager. I hadn't reached midlife yet. This is a time when a person is pressed on all sides. Small things begin to add up... years of lost privacy (toddlers banging on the bathroom door, rattling the handle, peeking through the keyhole), day after day of being endlessly available to shuttle kids, serve on church committees, clean and cook or work late hours for a corporation. Grandparents begin to need more care and attention. For the average person it's challenge enough; for the person driven to perfectionism and giving 200% it's a recipe for collapse, depression, flight or addiction—especially in the margins of life.

Wendell Berry says this about marginal land—that is, land that has less natural resources available (adequate rainfall, erosion barriers, and so forth): "... it is at the margins that the weaknesses of an enterprise will show first and most dramatically." The margins of a life can be different for different people; maybe the margin is one's relationship to children or spouse, maybe it is the ability to carry out necessary administrative tasks, or perhaps it is one's personal or physical wellbeing. Whatever is more fragile will begin to show the first signs of stress and failure; but these are only the early warning signs. Without strengthening the enterprise of one's life, stress can continue to travel inward, encroaching on seemingly fertile land, until the whole plot is eventually decimated. For the person who was able to promise the illusion of total presence and fertility before the pressures of life built up, infertility and disappearance become a real possibility.

---

2. And you?

In your journal, or during a small-group sharing time,
complete the thoughts:

"I tend to be someone who is prone to total involvement (separation);
for instance..."
"When I think about separating from people or work, I feel..."
"The margins of my life—the areas that come less easily for me—
are..."

If there was ever a book on presence, it is Song of Songs. Says the Lover to the Beloved in 7:6-9, "How fair and pleasant you are, O loved one, delectable maiden! You are stately as a palm tree, and your breasts are like its clusters. I say I will climb the palm tree and lay hold of its branches. O may your breasts be like clusters of the vine, and the scent of your breath like apples, and your kisses like the best wine that goes down smoothly, gliding over lips and teeth." Like I said, presence.

Yet in the middle of the book, the woman tries to sleep. No longer out in the sunshine, vineyards and orchards, she retreats to a seed-like place, quiet and dark in comparison, her energies unavailable. She closes the door, disrobes, bathes her feet. It is night, time for rest and dormancy. Still, the man comes knocking; when she does not answer, he thrusts his hand through the latch opening. It's an image of violation, even though the woman is filled with longing. When he flees, she goes out seeking him but is further violated by the night watchmen. What began as a hope for presence ends as degrading absence. The irony is that presence could have been preserved by the natural, built-in, absence and dormancy that night was supposed to provide. (Song of Songs, 5:2-7.)

Cycles in nature provide healthy rhythms of presence and absence that, overall, add up to fertility and perpetuation, ongoing presence. In spring the thorn flower is all ivory and lemon lace; by fall, it is tight red berries closed to honeybees and curious people like me. Similarly, a woman's body offers times of presence and absence. Leviticus supports this reality at the level of law, taking seriously the issue of blood as a signal of dormancy. It is easy to mistake these laws as statements about shamefulness, to interpret menstruation as a dirty, negative thing.

That's why Jesus is so shocking and refreshing. He too became absent from us, in death. He too claimed blood as the center of that absence. Then he asked the unthinkable, "Drink from it, all of you; for this is my blood...I tell you, I will never again drink of this fruit of the vine until that day when I drink it new with you in my Father's kingdom" (Matt. 26: 27-29). His departure and separation ultimately brings presence and communion. The cup he shares is filled with blood, communicating that true presence is entwined with absence; we have no part with him unless we embrace the irony by drinking.

When I consider this, set against the backdrop of Levitical law, it's as unthinkable today as it was to his disciples at the time ("This teaching is difficult; who can accept it?" (Jn. 6:60). It also causes me to question a common approach to "practicing presence," which is to continue thinking about God throughout the day, in an effort to keep him constantly available to our souls.

---

3. And you?

In your journal, or during a small-group sharing time, complete the thoughts:

"To me, dormancy is about..."

"In love and in work, I think absence can increase a sense of presence by..."

"The idea of absence from God being part of experiencing God's presence seems..."

In midlife, I began to understand addiction when I started blogging, Never struggling with smoke, drink, drugs, shopping, eating, I didn't know what all the fuss was about, but then what began as an experiment in career development consumed me. A sense of personal failure that had built up, and feelings of wanting to escape the overwhelming demands of family life, helped the medium overtake me. I blogged for hours (some of this was necessary for startup, but...), seven days a week, visiting my growing blogroll daily. If people commented on my blog, I always immediately returned the favor at their place. I posted every day, sometimes twice or in the middle of the night. I needed to be ever-present and when I was forced to be absent (darn those family vacations!), I apologized deeply to my community. While I was away, I ruminated about my absence, finding it hard to endure the separation.

I'd like to think I never developed a full-blown addiction (though my husband often teased me, asking, "So how's your Second Life?"). In a way, it doesn't matter. What matters is the picture I found in my study one night.

My daughter and I had decided to draw the Sermon on the Mount. I'd done my drawing first—a mountain, with items strewn along the path of ascent... necessary losses to achieve the climb towards open vistas. The next night I found her companion picture on our antique dressing table. Reflected in the mirror, I picked up the paper and noticed, amidst many kid-things, a rendition of a computer with a cup of tea beside it. My daughter does not drink tea beside a computer; she doesn't even use a computer. I saw my life through her eyes.

It took months for me to make changes. In some ways, I'm still making them, though my blog community will tell you I post less, comment less, and usually go away without telling them until I get back. To be adequately present in the long-term, I began to embrace absence. I don't know that my blogging friends experience this positively, if they sense my presence more keenly now that I've built a measure of absence into my online life. But I feel the freedom and grace of it deep down.

This experience, strangely perhaps, prepared me for the inevitable in my relationship with God. Beyond the cross, we still experience Divine advance and retreat, presence and absence, light and darkness, union and separation. So when the darkness began, I felt like I understood and wrote, "The night is a season, not the whole, just a slice. Like shadows that sometimes fall across the lawn, a small and transient space. I think too of tiny grooves in pine needles, slashes from end to end, slim depressions in which we travel for a brief time from one point to another."

To where do we travel? Night tends to slow us, ground us. In obscurity we can spread ourselves out, open our souls with a posture of renewed expectancy, focus and trust. Like Steven Chase says, "absence sharpens our seeking; it sets the tone and temper of our attentiveness." There in darkness, the Spirit leans in, poised for our lying down and sleep—a seed on a smooth slim stem, a red berry ripe for morning picking.

Playing towards God & discovery

I love this story from fellow blogger, Billy Coffey. It illustrates the delight of presence—sort of a *Song of Songs* on the highway. He relates...

Despite all the red lights, I should have been halfway home by now. I just happened to get stuck behind two people who consider a red light as the perfect excuse to kiss.

And boy, do these two know how to kiss.

It's been the same scenario every time—red light/brake/kiss/breathe/kiss. And then, a few moments after the light turns green, she pulls away and mouths I love you. He stares, not quite believing someone this special, this perfect, could ever say such words to someone like him.

To experience presence, the first requirement is to *show up*. We aren't going to get kissed in the car if we spend all our days puttering in the garage. The second requirement in experiencing presence is to provide moments to "breathe" ("brake/kiss/breathe /kiss").

Showing Up/Hiding: I will always remember my Grandmother, stretching in the morning. She used this exercise as a "time with God." Hands open to the sky, she invited his presence. Face to the ground, did she hide from him? I don't know all the details. No matter. You and I can create our own.

Choose a brief series of complementary stretches to do around the same time each day for the week. For instance, you might pair a "reach to the sky" stretch with a "hands to the ground" stretch or a "lean to the left" stretch with a "lean to the right" stretch. As you stretch, try to really feel the movement in your body. What does it feel like to move in one direction, then the opposite? Note the uniqueness of one sensation versus the other.

Now try to translate the sensations into emotions and thoughts. Does one direction make you feel happy and open? Does the other direction create tension or a sense of feeling closed or restful? Give these emotions and thoughts to God as you stretch. Or simply appreciate what the experience says to you about the two-sided reality of "presence" ("brake/kiss/ breathe/kiss").

Week 7 prayer

Lord, let me learn the rhythms of presence, which include seasons of absence. Let me not be afraid, but remember that you and I are always together, even when it seems we are apart.

Sabbath on the page

At least several times this week (or every day if you can swing it), try resting on the page by engaging in stream-of-consciousness writing. Do this for at least several pages. Consider writing nothing "spiritual" at all this week, and see what the experience is like. God may surprise you by his patience with such quietness on your part. And you might be surprised by this respite from trying to articulate spiritual things.

Blog it, to process and share

It's the end of week seven. Consider blogging about your experience. If you don't blog, you can do a "week-in-review" in your journal or write a letter to a friend or God. You could include:

• An idea that was new to you, or a quote you appreciated
• Something you liked about your experience

- Something you felt anxious or unsure about
- Any questions you have (no need to answer them; sometimes the asking is the most important step)
- Things you were reminded of: a story, memory, piece of art or music, bible verse or prayer, poem, current or historical event

Cycle: sabbath • week 8

...because it sets its own pace, [labor] is
usually accompanied by idleness, leisure, even sleep.

— Lewis Hyde

I go out at 10:00 pm, hour of raccoons and skunks. My heart beats fast. In darkness I become a magnet for sound. Rain *tap, tap, taps* or tree branches *crackle, crackle.* Things blur; water sounds like fire, melting ice like a wrapper opening. Visions of alternate realities push in... maybe I'm sitting under a giant toffee and creatures are nibbling through paper to bite sticky candy.

Smells of earth drift, and I notice them in ways I wouldn't notice during the day—openings, disintegrations, bloomings, fallings. My senses come alive to... I'm not sure what. I feel a purity of experience, unfettered by understanding and intention. Night speaks directly, and it's hard for me to get in the way. Is that why I feel afraid?

Day has its gifts, different. In the wee hours of morning there are special sights—dew beads suspended on grass, breath appearing against air even when it's not cold out. New light leans into wood-winged bushes and raspberries, casting long shadows. Stems arch, tip, ease into delightful homage. Amidst chatter, whistles, morning halloos, everything is opening. Silken threads hang, their whereabouts divulged by day.

I pick my way slowly, see that night did not abscond with the lawn. Here is the unmown grass. Here are the raspberries, webs, my own wet shoes and little humid circles of breath. The pine is right where I left her just yesterday.

~

It is enough to be raised in the household of an alcoholic. It'll do you, for developing issues around separation. But sometimes life offers the unsolicited double whammy. It did for me.

For many years, I thought of my parent's divorce as something that took my father away. But divorce researcher Judith Wallerstein suggests the loss goes deeper. She says children feel very small and frightened because the "family that created [them] simply vanished."

In the process of separation, something amorphous evaporates. Dad still exists. So does Mom. But the predictable circle of Mom-Dad dissipates. Apparently, even if parents are fighting like cats and dogs before the split, it doesn't matter much to the kids. There is security in the invisible "us," unhappy as it may be. (This does not include abuse of course, but is more about arguments, even heated ones.)

Prevailing wisdom has said that if the divorce is a "good one", this mitigates trauma; turns out it doesn't. Because, not only is family lost, but Mom (who's often keeper of the kids and supposed rock of support through divorce transition) is also lost. Wallerstein says that when the marriage falls apart, mom generally falls apart too, often becoming unable to offer the physical and emotional support she used to, to her kids. The loss of Mom's attention is, for young children, "unimaginably traumatic..."

I'm thinking age 3 counts as "young children." I know my mom did her best. She tucked me in at night, took me for walks to visit the old woman up the road, grew red roses and purple pansies and encouraged me to touch and smell them. She kept the wide-planked floors dusted and peeled oranges for us. But things had to be hard on her. Nights must've felt lonely. Maybe she cried herself to sleep. She wouldn't have purposely detached from us, but I'm guessing the divorce muted her ability to be present the way she'd been before.

---

1. And you?

In your journal, or during a small-group sharing time,

complete the thoughts:

"My early life experiences created a sense of security (loss); for example..."
"Divorce and/or alcoholism are issues I relate to (don't); after all..."
"Knowing that divorce and alcoholism could produce issues around separation, in children, helps me relate to myself (others); for instance..."

For me, loss stole a sense of trust that the world moves in predictable cycles. One day, Dad went away and never came back. Somehow, inexplicably, Mom went too. Not literally, but emotionally and mentally. Simple family cycles that could have built trust were derailed—dinner with the whole family, holidays spent side by side, evenings and mornings of family hugs.

On a practical level, such mistrust can breed a need for constant virility, making us one-sided personalities. True, some kids simply fall apart, but Elizabeth Marquardt notes that a good number of children-of-divorce become guards, bastions of strength, trying to keep life intact by acting like little adults. I suspect this greatly reduces the chance to try on both childhood and adulthood at will, through imagination and play. So not only do the larger cycles of family life disappear, but the personal patterns of give-and-take, exploration-of-strength versus weakness and so forth get pushed aside to meet the demands of a new reality.

If our ways of relating on a human level influence our ways of relating to God, then this is what life may look like for people like me: we fear cycles of presence and absence, we act strong, refuse rest, work extra hard, eschew play—mentally, emotionally, physically, and spiritually (though technically, these can't really be separated). Then, into this picture comes God, offering Sabbath. Doesn't he have a clue?

In Jewish Sabbath practice, no deliberate work, skill or craftsmanship is allowed. There are 39 categories of prohibited activities that seem based on the kind of labor that was necessary for Temple construction. But I like the way Nehemiah describes unacceptable Sabbath activity. He says, "In those days I saw in Judah people treading wine presses on the Sabbath, and bringing in heaps of grain and wine and loading them on donkeys; and also wine, grapes, figs, and all kinds of burdens, which they brought into Jerusalem on the Sabbath day..." (Neh 13:15)

I like Nehemiah's description because it focuses not so much on prohibition but the weight of reality. Words like *tread, heaps, loading, burdens* suggest a work-ethic that has gone beyond healthy productivity to bondage. Even the mention of donkeys stirs something in me, because a Jewish Sabbath made allowance for animals, including beasts of burden. So that Sabbath seems to say, to high and low, "Just stop. Tomorrow is another day. You will wake up and the press will still be there, the grain, the wine, the figs."

Lynne M. Baab, author of *Sabbath Keeping* notes that the Hebrew root for the word "Sabbath" includes "pause." To pause is to trust. It is to reframe presence-**absence** as presence-**hiddenness**—a fine line of distinction that speaks to the fear of permanent loss that our early loss experiences can create.

On the Sabbath, in an act of **hiding**, versus true **absence**, we draw a circle around a day, maybe by lighting a candle and saying a prayer and letting go. We veil our work for a time, the way night hides the things of day, and it is okay.

---

2. And you?

In your journal, or during a small-group sharing time,
complete the thoughts:

"In my background, I have experiences that have built (not built) a sense of life moving in cycles, such as..."

"I believe (don't believe) that our ways of relating on a human level influence our ways of relating to God, because..."

"To me, there's a difference (no difference) between absence and hiddenness, as characterized by..."

Letting go can be a scary prospect; maybe we can't imagine doing it because we've come to mistrust that life moves in cycles. Or maybe, and this is probably somehow related, we don't believe that hiddenness can be a partner to presence.

Sabbath is a weekly invitation to go nowhere, to believe that hiddenness is part of presence. I know that some say Sabbath is just about God, that it's not about resting up to be more productive, that it should not mean "nowhere goes somewhere" because we shouldn't be so focused on the "somewheres." But I believe that's exactly what Sabbath may be designed to do. Not in a simple cause and effect relationship, with productivity being the final goal, but more in the sense of rhythm that sees nowhere-somewhere, presence-hiddenness, as inextricably linked, with God on both sides of the dance.

The best analogy I can think of is my journey with poetry. I'm often asked for advice on how one can become a better poet. This assumes that becoming a better poet has something to do with writing better poems. It does. But becoming a better poet could also mean something apart from words on a page. It could mean being a person who really sees, who really hears and smells, tastes and touches. It could mean accepting the best in life and the worst as occasions to stand still, be silent and let the moments wash over us without feeling the need for interpretation. Becoming a better poet could mean developing a sense of compassion (the way those Israelites were supposed to have compassion for the donkeys). And yet there will always be a need to turn to words at some point, to give voice and form to what might otherwise go un-noticed by the world. In the end, it is impossible to define a poet as ei-ther/or. So, to be a better poet, one must speak and one must be silent, forge and stand idle, ride his figurative donkeys and tenderly settle them down to rest.

This is what Sabbath does. It is part of a cycle that teaches us to trust, making "nowhere" and "somewhere" unarguable partners. It reminds us not to be defined as either/or, allows us to try on different aspects of life at will. And this is freedom.

---

3. And you?

In your journal, or during a small-group sharing time, complete the thoughts:

"To me, Sabbath is about..."

"I tend to be defined by an either/or perspective in this area of my life..."

"For me, finding freedom might look like..."

We could celebrate Sabbath by embracing the 39 prohibitions. Or we might remember Nehemiah and the picture of bondage and go from there. To take the latter approach means more soul searching—as we consider what freedom might mean for us. What one person refrains from, another might embrace. For instance, when I began celebrating Sabbath (before working on this book, Sabbath mostly meant going to church!), I decided to forego writing on Sundays and dedicate part of the day to playing instruments. This has made room for the new pleas-ure of learning cello and the lost pleasure of fooling around on my flute.

So Sabbath frees me to be something other than "writer"; yet it also makes me more of a writer, as it develops unexplored parts of me that oddly impact my writing.

Then there's the matter of that blogging passion I mentioned before. When I considered my daughter's picture—the computer and teacup—I realized I'd begun to be one-sided. In my one-sidedness I was no longer free but was indulging my over-developed need for productivity, on the blogosphere stage. At some point, I determined that part of finding freedom would be to stop blogging on the Sabbath. So I stopped. Until the day I didn't.

On that day, as I walked away from the computer I said, as if to Someone, "So what?" A second later, I accidentally tipped a cup backwards and dumped water all over the keyboard. The event answered my question, "So what?" with a week of lost connection to the blogosphere. Ultimately, this is the problem with being one-sided; we lose connection to the very things we're trying to connect with. We fry our internal keyboards, so to speak, and are plunged into coerced silence and separation.

I always thought it was interesting that God told Israel he'd make up for the Sabbaths she'd broken, in a kind of coerced Sabbath situation (2 Chron. 36:21). For us, it may never be that dramatic or obvious. Maybe our kids will sadly draw pictures of teacups and computers behind our backs, wishing we'd find a Sabbath way of life. Or maybe we'll live feeling lost and tired, which makes us cranky, sick or in physical pain. Perhaps nothing will ever reach crisis proportions to force us into a compelled Sabbath, but we'll exist in a sort of limbo that isn't really life.

~

Morning never seemed that astonishing until I started going outside at night. By day's light, a world that had been hidden, just hours before, began to surprise me. Had the spiders always been here on these crystal-beaded webs? Had the tiny tear-shaped leaves of the thorn bush been yellowing like this every Fall— beginning the first soft weep of change? Likewise, night had seemed a simple end to day. Time to shut the door, flick the switches, make supper. But then I went out on starry nights and foggy nights, snowy and rainy nights. My senses woke to things that day, in her bustle and brilliance, had eclipsed. A variation of experience highlighted contrasts, deepening the separate experiences of sunup and sundown. One informed the other. In these changing contexts, I felt like a different person, more raw and attuned at night, more bold and curious by day. I became more comfortable trying on these different selves.

Still, when I wrote in my journal, "This year is about trust, that there is something deep within me that is going to meld with what is here in the woods..." I was only half right. This assumed that certain things existed in my heart that would find a parallel on the outside. On the matter of cycles and Sabbath, childhood losses made it hard to embrace a rhythm of presence-hiddenness that exists naturally in the little woods. It took evening and morning, the first day. And about 300 days on top of that, to even begin to restore what loss and fear had taken away. And, truth be told, I'm still not sure it was enough.

Playing towards God & discovery

I like this snippet of a story, told by author/blogger Gordon Atkinson. He says, "Wayne asked how the church was doing. I told him about our church. I admitted that we were a little unconventional, but only because we were committed to doing things the way that seemed right to us without regard for what was traditional among Baptists. Eventually the conversation turned toward our land and desire for our own building. 'I don't know. I'm not sure if we can grow large enough to afford a building. We're trying not to worry about numbers, but there are some undeniable mathematics involved here.'"

You can guess the end of the story. In the midst of undeniable mathematics, an unexpected equation came into view. In a way, this is how Sabbath works. One day out of seven, or 1=6 is an unexpected equation, but it seems to work miracles in our lives. Still, many of us have difficulty granting even one day of rest to our six days of work.

Just why do we shun giving up one day? Are we in need of claiming all the accomplishments for ourselves, when Sabbath suggests they might come from God and open space as well? Sabbath relieves us of our illusion and burden that we are the center of all our accomplishments.

Word Play Equation: Sentences, paragraphs, whole books, are made up of strange equations. The number of spaces, periods, exclamation points are not equal to the number of letters and words. The number of articles are not equal to the number of nouns. Yet the equations work to produce gifts of wisdom, insight, laughter. What if we changed the equations so radically that we eclipsed space, punctuation or varied wordforms altogether? Try it...

• type a whole paragraph of special thoughts, without space or punctuation. Ask someone else to read it. Discuss the experience.
• describe a beautiful experience using only three-letter words; share your piece with another person and see what she thinks of it

Few of us would dream of writing in the ways we just did. Yet we live our lives one-sidedly, without space and punctuation, variation. Perhaps we might consider a new equation that includes the simple addition of Sabbath to our weeks. It's just 1=6. What might you need to add or subtract, just one day a week, to experience freedom?

Week 8 prayer

God of the Universe, who created then rested, can you help me play life less one-sided and more whole?

Sabbath on the page

At least several times this week (or every day if you can swing it), try resting on the page by engaging in stream-of-consciousness **doodling**. Do this for at least several pages. The switch to **doodling** this week is a different experiment in Sabbath. We leave off from words to see what we might find in wordlessness.

Blog it, to process and share

It's the end of week eight. Consider blogging about your experience. If you don't blog, you can do a "week-in-review" in your journal or write a letter to a friend or God. You could include:

• An idea that was new to you, or a quote you appreciated
• Something you liked about your experience
• Something you felt anxious or unsure about
• Any questions you have (no need to answer them; sometimes the asking is the most important step)
• Things you were reminded of: a story, memory, piece of art or music, bible verse or prayer, poem, current or historical event

Poetry: silence • week 9

*Deeply listening to what is
within and around us changes us...*

— John Fox

This is what silence sounds like in my back yard...

...wind whooshing, woodpecker playing snare drum in the old maple, a yellow toy truck klunk-bashing tall cedar and jungle gym. Cordless drill making holes in someone's garage. Shouts, knocks, squeals, sirens, a harmonica. Hemlocks whisper-whispering, *shh, shh, shh, the girl can hear us.* Nuts cracking, water drip dripping. Leaf blowers, lawn mowers, an ice cream truck blaring electric-sick rendition of *You are My Sunshine.* A plane roaring towards Chicago, or maybe Africa. An aluminum door banging, playing hard-to-get with the breeze (*you can have me, no you can't*). The dog next door, first in a game of dog dominoes, woof-woof-woof down the street and back again and again and again.

I take what I can get.

~

In a way, I'm grateful my silence opportunities are semi-urban. I'm not sure I could handle sheer silence the way journalist Rory Stewart did, as he walked through days of it across parts of Afghanistan —no woodpeckers drumming on their drums, no kids hurling toy trucks at trees... just the sounds of his own breathing, shoes crunching gravel, backpack chafing, "phuh, phuh, phuh."

Silence makes you attentive to the tiniest sound underfoot, helps you hear the pulse of your heart, reminds you of the burden flapping on your back. If God were to show up and speak, like he did to Elijah after the wind died down and the silence ensued, you might have a chance to hear God's voice. Unfortunately, we're culturally primed to avoid silence. Stuart Sim, in his article "Sssshhhh..." notes that our culture's business ethic is driven by noise. For instance, bars purposely drown out talk to increase alcohol consumption. Sim concludes, "Never forget, noise sells, and in a consumer society that's the bottom line."

Yet bars and businesses aren't the only place where noise reigns. We invite a constant stream of sound through the use of, among other gadgets, the ubiquitous cell phone. To this, Lauren Winner recounts an informal experiment she did while walking across campus; she observed that most people, whether alone or in groups, were talking on cell phones. In stark contrast to Rory Stewart's silent trek, we "stroll... talking into tiny bits of plastic—and most of what we're saying is pretty lame. ('Well, I'm about 10 seconds from the library... yep, now I'm walking up the library steps... no, okay, well here I am entering the library, I'll see you in three seconds.')." Winner concludes, "Solitude is scary, but scarier still is the prospect of a society in which no one has time to be quiet, to be reflective."

Having grown up in a difficult household, I keenly understand our societal shyness regarding silence. People have different reasons for avoiding the quiet; in my case, silence was often punishing. My stepfather would descend into months where he refused to address us, and at the same time we were left to judge the true nature of his mood (would he hide the car keys today, should we scurry to the safety of our bedrooms to avoid the flinging of a plate?) The painful silence was exacerbated, since he would entertain outside friends around the table, sharing beer, stories and laughter, while he looked straight through us without a word.

Quite young, I learned to fill the silence with my own sound. My paternal grandfather called me "chatter-box." Today, my husband likes to bring me along in social situations, because I know how to keep a conversation going. And yet. This same quality can be a barrier to relationship with God and others.

---

1. And you?

In your journal, or during a small-group sharing time, complete the thoughts:

"I would define silence as..."
"I can find silence by..."
"The last time I found silence was..."

"Listening is the path to intimacy," says poet John Fox. But what if we are wired for sound, whether out of pain or personality?

Many spiritual practices like silence seem unfairly slanted towards the healthy introvert. Take a Sabbath? No problem for the shy guy who's been dealing with meetings and cafeteria chit-chat all week and can't wait for a dose of home-alone. Quiet meditation on Scripture? Cool deal for the girl who dreaded reading out loud in class on Tuesday. Breath prayer, contemplative prayer, centering prayer... marvelous methods for those of few words. Silence? Bring it on, says the happy introvert.

This is not to suggest that people-of-words who have issues around loss and separation shouldn't practice Sabbath, meditation, or silence. But it's not going to come easily. Recently, I was made temporarily hopeful on the silence issue when a chiropractor told me, "I'm going to adjust your mouth." I laughed out loud and told her I wished it was as simple as that. Equally promising was a method I read about, used by some desert saint. To overcome gossip and frivolous talk, he carried a stone in his mouth. Effective as it probably was, I figured if I tried it I'd end up with bite-imbalance, and this would land me back at the chiropractor.

What's a dysfunctional extrovert to do?

Besides sitting outside in semi-urban quietude, I've found unexpected silence-and-listening practice through poetry. You can tell when a poet has been a good listener, because the poem is more likely to capture the essence of a thing, more likely to reproduce its voice and the heart of its rhythms; it also tends to reveal dreams and burdens that may exist in the poet or the poet's community.

To become better poet-listeners, Fox suggests that we quiet ourselves for a good ten minutes and practice listening to the world around us. With the openness of a contemplative, we're to make note of movement sounds, voice sounds, doors shutting, dogs barking. Then he suggests we focus on one or two of the sounds that most intrigue us. Feel them, he instructs. Note *where* you feel them in your body.

---

2. And you?

In your journal, or during a small-group sharing time, complete the thoughts:

"I agree (disagree) that many spiritual practices seem slanted towards the 'healthy introvert'..."

"Listening is (is not) the path to intimacy, because..."

"If I close my eyes and listen right now, I hear..."

Such exercise in listening produces surprising intimacy. Like the day I decided to listen to a Coke bottle. I'm kind of a health nut; I can't remember the last time I took a swig of soda. But I listened anyway and this is the poem I found when I quieted myself…

"Bottled"

I am fizzle
fazzle pizzazz,
snap crackle…
slide your hand
past my red belt
take me by the
ribbed neck
set teeth on edge
flick fluted tin
and, pop!

We can question the value of bonding with a Coke bottle by listening to it, then writing down what we hear. But I like to remember Ruth Haley Barton's observation that we bring the same patterns of intimacy to our relationship with God that we have with people (and, I would add, with the created and invented world around us). In other words, if I can't bond with a Coke bottle for ten minutes, or imagine what it is like to be a Coke drinker, I'm less likely to be able to bond with an invisible God. The interesting thing about the soda poem is that it led one commenter (I posted the poem on my blog) to suddenly desire a Coke; it urged another commenter to admit a questionable habit (his value judgment, not mine) of opening bottle tops with his teeth. This is how it works when we get intimate; a process of identification and sharing is initiated.

King David, great poet of the bible, was a pretty good listener. He listened to sky, wind, deer, cattle, mountains, valleys, cedars and goats. In their rising, panting, going in and coming out, he heard echoes of the Divine, and responded, "O LORD, how manifold are your works! In wisdom you have made them all; the earth is full of your creatures." This led him to uninhibited praise: "I will sing to the LORD as long as I live; I will sing praise to my God while I have being" (Ps. 104:24, 33).

Writing poetry can lead us to intimacy and praise; it can also help us begin to listen to ourselves. It's a kind of active silence well-suited to the extrovert, wherein we welcome flapping sounds from the burden on our backs and express them in the space of a poem. The confines of limited space ask us to first listen hard, so we can later capture and powerfully communicate elusive truth. As Fox notes, the point is not to become a world-famous poet (a daunting goal indeed) but rather to provide "a home for your bewilderment. A healing place for your anger... the space [you] need to breathe and wander, laugh and wail."

Is this why the Psalms have been one of the most enduring and inviting parts of the bible? What David pulled from the depths of his soul on silent nights, are poetic truths so raw, ebullient, furious, and sorrowful, that we can taste the truth of his experience. His words help us become intimate with ourselves, others and God by providing a home for our confusion, a healing place for our disillusionment, a place to breathe. In the end, I can think of no better way to express what poetry, including David's poetry, does for us than to share these words from poet Laure Krueger. In an intimate act of listening to my words of disillusionment in an online post, she juggled and reformed them into this...

i find myself thirsty
for plain sounds that whisper,
glory.
sure words resonate
where i can hear, once again,
God moving

through broken lines
that murmur with tenderness. but
at the heart of poetry,
silences.

I'm not offering an "Arnoldian notion of poetry replacing religion," but rather a recognition that God murmurs in the silence of unexpected places. Poetry can be one of those places.

---

3. And you?

In your journal, or during a small-group sharing time, complete the thoughts:

"Listening depends on (does not depend on) hearing sounds..."
"I feel comfortable (uncomfortable) with the idea of writing poetry as a way to listen, because..."
"I think God could (could not) murmur through the silence of poetry, because..."

I'd love to see more people practice silence through the reading and writing of poetry, and hopefully I've convinced a few people through my enthusiasm. Still, I'm reminded of my efforts to study French. I considered translating sections of the bible, which is how I learned a good deal of Spanish. And I had some success using magazines and children's books. But then someone gave me a book of French poetry. My passion for verse set me to translating with great interest and consistency; I'm learning French faster now because I found my translating sweet spot.

Sitting in a quiet prayer closet might be your silence sweet-spot. But maybe you'd fare better with an active approach to silence... if not writing poetry, then perhaps drawing. Walking alone is good. You might go fishing without your iPod®. I can also recommend reclining on a sunny day and listening to a good game of dog dominoes.

I can't guarantee that silence, or any of the spiritual practices, will change you in all the ways you'd like. But life might not be about becoming perfect, pleasing everybody all of the time and never disappointing God with our intimacy shortcomings. At least that's what I started to think along the way.

Playing towards God & discovery

When you are in silence, there is still sound. Your role is to listen. What does it mean to listen? It is different than simple hearing; it means to *pay attention, wait attentively or in suspense, to tune in*. As we tune in, we are made more ready to place our discoveries into poetry.

Not all poems we write will necessarily speak about God. Remember the Coke bottle poem? It said nothing of God, but writing about the bottle required attentiveness and openness to discovery, a focusing on particular truths which could itself be understood as a form of spiritual expression. As long as we write from a place of discovery, nothing will be lost.

Listen to the Morning: Consider trying this every morning for the week. Sit outside or near an open window. Using all five senses, listen to the morning. Write it down in no particular order. For instance, this is what I am hearing in my morning: wind in the trees sounds like a rain stick, birds "shweet, shweet," a child calls for his mother, sun dances on the hemlocks, Provencal yellow cotton tablecloth sits soft beneath my elbow, "clicketty, clicketty, clicketty" says my keyboard, a crow "caw, caws," smell of charcoal and fresh cut grass comes in on the breeze, green tea from Granada has a hint of flowers and honey.

Now make a simple poem. Don't worry about form or meaning. Just begin, like this...

Morning comes,
a rain stick dancing
with sun on hemlocks.
"Caw, caw," cries the
crow. Maybe he wishes
for softness of French
yellow cloth or sip of
flowery green tea. He will
have to settle for clicketty,
clicketty: just me, tapping
out his morning wishes.

You can also take your morning listening and put it into different frameworks. The *The Making of a Poem: The Norton Anthology of Poetic Forms* gives a good introduction to *form poetry*, which you can experiment with as a place to put what you "hear." Another great reading resource, to see models, is *The Poets' Book of Psalms: The Complete Psalter as Rendered by Twenty-Five Poets from the Sixteenth to the Twentieth Centuries.*

Week 9 prayer

Lord, who hovered over the waters in silence before speaking words, teach me to listen before I respond.

Sabbath on the page

At least several times this week (or every day if you can swing it), try resting on the page by engaging in stream-of-consciousness writing. Do this for at least several pages. If you like, incorporate what you "hear" from the room in which you write. Don't feel the need to respond, just record.

Blog it, to process and share

It's the end of week nine. Consider blogging about your experience. If you don't blog, you can do a "week-in-review" in your journal or write a letter to a friend or God. You could include:

• An idea that was new to you, or a quote you appreciated
• Something you liked about your experience
• Something you felt anxious or unsure about
• Any questions you have (no need to answer them; sometimes the asking is the most important step)
• Things you were reminded of: a story, memory, piece of art or music, bible verse or prayer, poem, current or historical event

Me: selfcare • week 10

There cannot be a stressful crisis next week.
My schedule is already full.

— Henry Kissinger

The woods are full of webs. Who knew there were so many spiders spinning, on any given day? I have seen a silken hourglass keeping time with grains of pollen. Too, there was the single thread hanging from pine, like fishing line cast to catch some fish foolish enough to swim on air. Some threads hang in bushes, capture bronzed needles, petals, leaves—create makeshift mobiles that could entertain a stray baby, should he show up in need of a diversion.

When new light slants through these woods just right, I can see fine streamer webs, which extend from hemlocks... ten, fifteen, sometimes twenty feet over the yard—made by party spiders, no doubt, who choose to decorate the day with a wave of simple thread, anchored only on one side, riding on air, loose, free.

Engineer spiders live here too. These are the builders of suspension bridges, elegant lines that extend flat from dogwood to wood-winged bush, with slender cables draped from above. They connect one place to another, cross chasms, hope to lure a beetle traveler looking for some shortcut.

If a mischievous fairy godmother turned me into a spider tomorrow, I'm guessing I'd turn up as the engineer type, building bridges. Or maybe I would just become the web itself... suspended over a rift valley.

~

Kissinger was being witty when he said he couldn't handle an unexpected crisis "next week" because his schedule was already full. And yet.

For those of us who feel we must be The One to handle everything, that's not how it goes. No kidding around. Our schedules might be full, but we *are going to handle* the next crisis. *We have to,* or so we believe. Otherwise the world might fall apart.

Once, I wrote a poem about such things. The words bubbled from my own place of fear that began to surface during my year outdoors: *if I don't hold the world together, who will?*

The poem is called "Stayed: for Ann Voskamp."

Why do we not
leave home.
Is it really for fear
of what lies
beyond, or rather
for fear that the
roof will abscond
with the doors
and the shutters
we've always known.
And who would they
blame if it happened
just so, if the whole
curtained place simply
picked up its stakes,
disappeared on the wind
in our absence. What
are we really afraid
of, why do we not
leave home.

There are different reasons we might believe we need to be the center of everything, hold the world together. Some of us are do-ers by personality. It's actually part of our talent, to handle things with a clear eye, to be the first to step up. But some of us come to this place through painful experiences. (And a few of us have the "blessing" of both!)

---

1. And you?

In your journal, or during a small-group sharing time, complete the thoughts:

"I feel (don't feel) the need to handle things all the time, for instance..."
"I am comfortable (uncomfortable) letting others hold the world together sometimes, because..."
"I tend (don't tend) to sacrifice my needs for the needs of others, maybe because..."

When I look at personality themes in tests like *StrengthsFinder*, I find I'm triple-A: Achiever, Activator, Arranger. Then there are the realities of my past.

Divorce books put it like this: when a couple splits, kids often serve the role of *bridge*. 'Mom-n-dad', formerly a one-phrase entity, are now two entities separated by a chasm. Children stand in the gap, protecting one parent from the other, keeping secrets one from the other, assuaging the feelings of each, and generally holding on for dear life to both sides of the rift. They sacrifice their needs for the illusion of keeping the family together.

Similarly, people who live with drinkers tend to subsume their needs, their wishes, to the urgent task of holding reality together. Melody Beattie notes that not only do we reality-preservers ignore our needs, we often don't even know them. When they surface on occasion, we tend to see them as wrong or bad, so we push them aside again. And, anyway, we become used to not getting our needs met through the vagaries of the situation.

Is this why I came to my own internal crisis? Catalyzed by a simple commitment to sit in the woods for a year? Maybe.

Looking back, I see how it went. I thought the true crisis was the one that brought me to the woods to fix myself. I had come feeling limited, looking for a way to forget those feelings of limitation. Furthermore, certain relationships were showing strain and struggle. I took most of the blame, accepting the burden of failure. *I am selfish, mean, a bad person in need of serious change.*

Was this the whole story?

---

2. And you?

In your journal, or during a small-group sharing time,
complete the thoughts:

"I would describe myself as someone who knows (doesn't know) his/her needs, because..."
"I tend to judge my needs and dreams as bad (good), for instance..."
"The last time I felt in crisis was... I can see that it was about..."

There were days when I would come to the woods and think, *what's the point... I'm wasting my time... nothing is happening here... I'm not doing*

anything.... And then maybe the back door would pop open and somebody would tell me I was needed. It was the phone. Or a lost shoe.
Strawberries needed cutting. Something. Then my guilt would
heighten. Who did I think I was sitting out here doing *nothing*? This is
just the kind of thing a selfish, mean, bad person would do, when all
around her the world was in need.

These feelings were the tip of the iceberg. Who did I think I was
being a writer? A speaker? Spending time alone to get my head together,
spending time away to get my career together? Who was going to hold
this family together, if not me? One night I made my decision. I would
give it all up. Everything. Shut down my blogs. Stop writing. Quit going
to conferences. Then everything would be okay. Wouldn't it?

It would. It had to be. I'd always been the person who tried to play
the part of *bridge*, who tried to hold things together. I would be that
person now, even if it killed me.

As I made the decision, I could feel the dying start, almost like a
physical feeling, an emptiness opening inside. Well and good, this was
a sign of Christian life. This was what spiritual practice was designed to
do... help us die to ourselves. (Did it matter that soon after I also toyed
with the idea of never eating again? A silly idea of course, for someone
who loves food as much as I do, but fantasies aren't always sensible.)

I forgot, in all my dying, to give up the reading of poetry. And that
is a dangerous thing.

One day I read "To You," by Walt Whitman. Because of the title,
I felt a pointedness about the message. It's a long poem, so I'll only
share part of it...

> *... now I place my hand upon you, that you be my poem;*
> *I whisper with my lips close to your ear,*
> *I have loved many women and men, but I love none better than you.*
> *...*
> *O I could sing such grandeurs and glories about you!*

You have not known what you are—you have slumber'd upon yourself
all your life;
Your eye-lids have been the same as closed most of the time...

The mockeries are not you;
Underneath them, and within them, I see you lurk;
I pursue you where none else has pursued you;
Silence, the desk, the flippant expression, the night, the accustom'd
routine, if these
conceal you from others, or from yourself, they do not conceal you
from me...

The hopples fall from your ankles—you find an unfailing sufficiency...
Through angers, losses, ambition, ignorance, ennui, what you are
picks its way.

Sometimes a poem is just a poem. But sometimes it is an unexpected messenger. For me, these words from Whitman felt like an odd valentine from God, along the lines of Psalm 139:14, "I am fearfully and wonderfully made." Maybe I was worth taking care of after all?

---

3. And you?

In your journal, or during a small-group sharing time,
complete the thoughts:
"I feel needed to do things like..."
"I would like to give up doing..."
"A small way I could begin taking care of myself might be..."

Acting as *bridge* puts strain on our souls. Always being the one to handle things, neglecting our needs and dreams to stand in some supposed gap in the lives of friends and family causes stress. Over time, we risk breakdown, physical or mental, the way I realize I'd started to collapse, as evidenced by the things that first brought me out to the little woods.

Yet we're sometimes tempted to respond by giving up even more. It's a strategy we've used for so long, and it seems quite spiritual on the surface. But Parker Palmer says this, "Self-care is never a selfish act—it is simply good stewardship of the only gift I have, the gift I was put on earth to offer others." In other words, if I die inside (or worse, if that leads me to act that out physically), I will have lost any opportunity to truly care for others.

We don't need to start big in this self-care thing. Small opportunities come every day, chances to step back and let others take the reins, while we go off and find respite. Once I began looking, I found these chances in the simplest ways. Like the night I asked my eleven-year-old to make salad by herself for the first time. With a chef's knife. And lettuce. Cucumber and condiments.

I put my coat on, walked out the back door and picked my way to the little woods. Sitting on the sled I thought, "What if she cuts her thumb? What if she drops the knife and it stabs her toe? It could happen. Anything could happen."

Like a voyeur of salad-makers, I watched my daughter through the window. She moved from one task to the next. Lettuce into the bowl, clean and ripped. Cucumber sliced. No apparent uprisings from the produce. Olive oil. Balsamic vinegar. Spice. No mutiny staged by the condiments.

You mean I could take some time for myself, while other people stepped in to take responsibility? So it seemed. My daughter reaped a different benefit, making her very first salad alone. With a knife, without me.

The moment called for a poem...

Moon shimmers, glassy blue
night. I lie under glistening
pine, watch house lights shine
over empty white yard while my
girl cuts cucumber crescents
on grain-gold kitchen counters.

Such small acts of self-care can prepare us for moments when the stakes seem higher: we need to go away for a week and not just to the back yard for fifteen minutes on a moonlit night. In the bigger moments, guilt might press even harder, and maybe the relational systems in which we exist will push harder too. It won't be easy, but we've been reaching towards this. Besides, it's not just about our freedom; there are benefits that others are waiting for too, even if they don't know it quite yet.

~

For the wounded who struggle with self-care, Calhoun recommends AA, Al-Anon, and divorce-recovery workshops. I also recommend a year outdoors, dangerous poetry, and Psalm 139. That, or we can bribe our fairy godmothers: *turn me into a party spider, free to dress the day in streamers.* Now, if I could just figure out when to party and when to bend...

Playing towards God & discovery

Stress is more than an unpleasant feeling. It has deep consequences, as it can destroy brain cells, depress immune response, encourage heart attack and stroke and impair learning. It's not like spiritual life never calls us to stressful situations, but if we bring constant stress on ourselves by playing martyr in our relationships, then we cause unwarranted damage that can eventually affect our personal health and the health of our relationships.

Bridge Building: Make two stacks of books of the same height, with a gap of about 8 inches between them. Using a piece of unfolded paper, bridge the gap by simply setting each end on one stack of books. Does the paper stay? Place a penny on the paper. What happens?

Now, take the paper and put two folds in it the long way, so your paper looks like a large U. Place it over the books again. How many pennies can you set on it before it buckles?

Try the same experiment using other folding methods or adding supports under the paper. Can it hold more pennies, without collapsing? At what point do you need to stop adding pennies, to preserve the bridge?

Life Bridge: Consider your life. What are the various "pennies"? Name them in your journal. Who is placing them on you? Is it time to say no to certain "pennies"? Sometimes it may be necessary to refuse to play the bridge; however, you might also find ways to re-form or support yourself to serve in that role. If you like, sketch some ideas for re-forming or supporting yourself.

For more on how to make choices and organize your life in a healthy way, check out Ruth Haley Barton's *Sacred Rhythms*, particularly the chapters on "Discernment" and "Rule of Life" (which Barton prefers to reframe as "cultivating rhythms"); the secular, albeit sometimes reductive book, *The Power of Less* might also be helpful.

Week 10 prayer

God of Creation, you exist in a give-and-take trinity of relationship.

Teach me the mystery of being fully myself, even as I love and live in community.

Sabbath on the page

At least several times this week (or every day if you can swing it), try resting on the page by engaging in stream-of-consciousness writing. Do this for at least several pages. Take this time for yourself. It will make you a calmer, more thoughtful person when approaching the day and others.

Blog it, to process and share

It's the end of week ten. Consider blogging about your experience. If you don't blog, you can do a "week-in-review" in your journal or write a letter to a friend or God. You could include:

• An idea that was new to you, or a quote you appreciated
• Something you liked about your experience
• Something you felt anxious or unsure about
• Any questions you have (no need to answer them; sometimes the asking is the most important step)
• Things you were reminded of: a story, memory, piece of art or music, bible verse or prayer, poem, current or historical event

With: submission • week

Only strength can cooperate. Weakness can only beg.

— *Dwight D. Eisenhower*

On cold days, I see steam from my teacup. It is a scarf held by an invisible hand. Vapor undulates, as if some Bolero song teases it onward, upward. Perhaps this show of air and steam will rouse the prickly pine from her slumber.

How intimate the dance, much like trees and wind. When air flows over the landscape, the pine wakens, speaks. Maples, touched, whisper like a thin layer of ice crackling, or the feet of miniature creatures scurrying into the sky.

Kale, blue green, bends beneath remnants of last night's rain. It is heavy with golden fingers of seed pods. Raspberry bushes arch, long arms reaching towards the lawn, delivering little red baskets that bob like the bottoms of hot air balloons readying to touch down to earth.

And the tiny white moth rises from grass. It carries light on its wings like a barely-there grace. Leaves drift and swirl on eddies of warm air. I close my eyes. I'm a wisp on the wind, now diving past the neighbor's dog (a near collision), then on again over the grey house, flying with sparrows. Something inside me feels like fire, a sure melting, a merging with Spirit I sense in beauty. All this beauty, laid out on a postage-stamp-sized piece of property, a party spilling past bushes and chain link fence.

~

We sit down to dinner and the narrative begins. "Ricky!" my younger daughter Sonia begins. Then, beat by beat, we are treated to the most recent episode of *I Love Lucy* she watched and absorbed. Sonia mimics so carefully that, instead of seeing my brown-haired girl, I see a red-head with pouty lips and enough mascara to supply the whole neighborhood.

It's the way my daughter moves, the tone, the just-right opening of eyes in surprise. Lucy's come to supper.

I'm not much of an actress myself, but I know a thing or two about mimicking (a quality that on the surface seems much like submission). It's a skill that kids of divorce pick up along the way, as they pay close attention to the different rules in their respective parent's homes. In order to keep from seeming too much like mom (for dad) and too much like dad (for mom), kids mimic each parent closely and adjust themselves on the spot, shaping and reshaping beliefs and habits on demand. For this reason, Marquardt notes, kids of divorce often feel like different people with each of their parents.

These dynamics are remarkably similar to the those in the alcoholic household, where family members learn to do things they don't want to, say yes when they mean no, do things for others that they could just as well do for themselves, meet people's needs before asked, fix others' feelings. They think ahead for people, speak for them even. It's often done in a friendly manner that presumes to be submissive caretaking.

While considering the nature of true submission, I happened to spend a day with a person who engaged in a kind of caretaking that shadowed and mimicked. This person drove me just about crazy, and I suddenly understood why one of my best friends had once said, "You're so hard to live with." I think what that person meant was, "You're driving me just about crazy with all this pseudo-submission." Because, of course, it ends up feeling to the recipient like a kind of neurotic control. At least that's how I felt when I spent the day with Caretaker Woman. I wished I could read her this passage from *Eat, Pray, Love*...

Letting go, of course, is a scary enterprise for those of us who believe that the world revolves only because it has a handle on top of it which we personally turn, and that if we drop the handle for even a moment, well—that would be the end of the universe. But try dropping it... Sit quietly for now and cease your relentless participation. Watch what happens. The birds do not crash dead out of the sky in mid-flight, afer all. The trees do not wither and die... Life continues to go on... Why are you so sure that your micromanagement of every moment in this whole world is so essential? Why don't you let it be?

Of course, I didn't read this passage to Caretaker Woman. But I did go home full of questions after our day together. So, was this what it felt like to be on the other side? When my kids put a glass on the counter and I reached out and moved it an inch, just because? Or when they came to the end of their dinner and I had to ask if they wanted more food, before they could even consider within themselves whether or not they were still hungry? Was this what it felt like when I intervened in my in-laws conflict with their kid in a restaurant? How about the seemingly generous questions, "Can I get that for you? What do you need? What are you doing... I mean, if you tell me, I can help."

---

1. And you?

In your journal, or during a small-group sharing time, complete the thoughts:

"I feel like it's okay (not okay) to shape and reshape our behavior depending on who we're with, because..."
"The last time I engaged in caretaking, it looked like..."
"When others take care of me, I prefer it to look like..."

I don't blame myself. Life experience brought me to this place of pseudo-submission. And I wasn't entirely comfortable with the results. I'd felt the confusion Beattie says caretakers often feel, as well as the anxiety, frustration and discontent. Worst of all, I'd felt the anger. She says, "Caretaking breeds anger. Caretakers become angry parents, angry friends, angry lovers." Yup.

If there's one thing I like about Jesus, it's his cool-as-a-cucumber demeanor. Apparently, if there was any stray dysfunction in his house, it didn't make an impact. He always seemed to know exactly who he was and what he wanted. He knew when to submit and when to walk away. Or maybe I should say he knew *how* to submit. Because, like Adele Calhoun says, "Sometimes submission means giving. Sometimes it means receiving. Sometimes submission means leading and at other times it means following. But in each case there is an element of self-giving."

In other words, we've been handed a problematic vocabulary to describe this practice. 'Sub' means 'under.' But true submission is more like the *art of working with* a person or situation, the way the steam from my teacup works with the breeze. And why would we want to engage in this art? For the purpose of putting on the best life-party possible.

Jesus understood this at Cana. When his mother made a request that didn't fit with his schedule of divine revelation, he made a judgment. He decided to work with the situation, to work with her and the servants who were standing by waiting for instructions. So the water became wine—so rich in flavor that even the intoxicated guests woke to its presence (Jn. 2). At Gethsemane, he similarly decided to work with the crowd. They came with clubs and swords and were thrown backwards when he answered, "I am." But in the end, for the love of you and me and so many more, he subdued his power so they could manage to stand, and he walked with them through the night (Jn. 18:6).

This same Jesus, standing before Pilate, seemed oddly subversive (Mk. 15:4). John Leax reflects on why Jesus refused to speak. He observes that Jesus' "refusal to speak at such a moment must be more than a rhetorical ploy. Surely he is not deliberately angering Pilate... I think

Jesus is silent because he is the Christ, because he stands before Pilate the embodiment of truth, the Word made flesh. No word uttered in a human tongue could contain the reality of his presence." We could say that in this case Jesus worked *with* the truth, and essentially he worked *with* Pilate too, answering the desperate question lurking in the governor's heart ("What is truth?" in John 18:38). So, real submission has no formulaic face. It can look like acquiescence or it can look like rebellion. But its center is a love that works *with*.

---

2. And you?

In your journal, or during a small-group sharing time, complete the thoughts:

"When I do things for others I feel..."
"*The art of working with* seems like (doesn't seem like) a plausible way to frame submission, because..."
"To me, working *with* the truth feels exciting (scary), because..."

As a child, I watched my mother "submit" to my stepfather. She cooked hamburgers almost every night, because that's what he wanted, even though she didn't like hamburgers much. She made us sit silent at the dinner table because he said children were to be seen and not heard; I still remember the occasional pinch on my leg, a signal to clam up. One day, when my stepfather had a friend over and they'd been drinking for a while, my mother submitted to his order to give the drunken friend a pancake that had just been partially eaten by our dog. Sure, the friend was asking for the pancake; in his intoxicated state he didn't know any better, but my mom sure did. She submitted to a lot of other things too, maybe because my stepfather was such a volatile man.

Is it any wonder then, even though I learned how to pseudo-submit, as a child of divorce and alcoholism, I also came to despise the thought of *consciously submitting*? Once, I wrote a poem about my fears regarding the whole issue. It was called "Statue in the Rain." It captured my view of what it meant to be in relationship: the statue gradually lost its features to years of pelting water and hungry moss. Identity was stripped away. The elements won, the statue lost. Maybe that's why I had to try practicing real submission, the Jesus kind. It seems a whole lot more dignified, in my opinion, as it flows from a deep sense of self-in-God that is tough to erode.

I don't know if anyone has noticed my efforts. They might just have to take my word for it. But there are things that go unsaid these days. Questions don't get asked, like "What are you doing? What do you need?" Water glasses get set down and I don't move them. Dinners come and go, where I wait for people to serve themselves again if they decide, on their own, that they are hungry. Friends struggle and I don't reach out to rescue them. Or, if a situation seems to truly warrant help, maybe I do. I say no to some things I used to say yes to and vice versa. People make wrong turns and I let them. Other times, I bridge a gap even though it's uncomfortable, because I realize that's what I need to do, not out of neediness but out of a consciousness that to do so would be a life-giving act of working *with*.

This kind of submission is both harder and easier, but it's what I want now that I've thought it through. Have I perfected it yet? No, but I'm thinking that might be okay.

---

3. And you?

In your journal, or during a small-group sharing time,

complete the thoughts:

"Someone I admire who is good at 'working with' others is..."
"When I think about what that person does in those moments, I would describe it like..."
"The last time I 'worked with' someone in a situation was.... It felt..."

~

Some days in January, when ice is hanging on branches and snow is knee-deep, I become a child again, willing to work with the landscape. I break an icicle and suck it, gather snow in a cupped hand and munch it. I sip tea, red or green, that I've brought to this little woods, watch steam do her dance and I long for the freedom to seamlessly connect. When my time outdoors comes to a close, I put the sled at hill's crest and decide I am not, after all, too old to work with gravity. Whoosh! I am off, laughing, laughing. The life of the party.

Playing towards God & discovery

How do we get to the place where we want to work with others? It flows not only from trust but also from a deep-rooted admiration. Developing trust can take a long time. Cultivating admiration might be an easier place to begin. This is probably done most easily first with objects. Once you develop the habit of admiration, it's not so hard to begin admiring people more deeply as well.

Make it Beautiful: Choose one object to focus on for the week. In your journal, sketch the object. Each day, sketch it from a different angle. Try sketching it in different lights or in different settings. If you prefer to write about the object, then write about it. Note its unique qualities. Try touching and smelling the object, or producing sound with it. Are you brave? Why not taste it too? After sketching or writing about the object, put it away. Sketch or describe the empty space that is left in its stead.

Put it in Psalm 104 (NRSV): Each day, when you are finished observing, sketching or describing your object, you can place it in the context of God's creative love. Psalm 104:14-23 essentially admires God's works as a way of worshiping God. Read this section of the Psalm and find a place to tuck in your object and a few of its qualities. Then write the Psalmist's response next to your original sketch or description: "O LORD, how manifold are your works! In wisdom you have made them all; the earth is full of your creatures" (Ps. 104:24).

Verse 13 of the same Psalm declares to God, "the earth is satisfied with the fruit of your work." God's love and admiration of his creation causes him to work *with* and *for* it. Your admiration can help you do the same, for others and the world.

Week 11 prayer

God of Nurture, the earth is satisfied with the fruit of your work. Through grace, let me also satisfy others and the world with the fruit of mine.

Sabbath on the page

At least several times this week (or every day if you can swing it), try resting on the page by engaging in stream-of-consciousness writing. Do this for at least several pages. As you find a sense of greater calm and insight through this simple exercise, don't be surprised if you are enabled to more easily *work with* others.

Blog it, to process and share

It's the end of week eleven. Consider blogging about your experience. If you don't blog, you can do a "week-in-review" in your journal or write a letter to a friend or God. You could include:

• An idea that was new to you, or a quote you appreciated
• Something you liked about your experience
• Something you felt anxious or unsure about
• Any questions you have (no need to answer them; sometimes the asking is the most important step)
• Things you were reminded of: a story, memory, piece of art or music, bible verse or prayer, poem, current or historical event

Home: hospitality • week 12

Hospitality is a state of mind, not a prescriptive agenda...

— *Duchess*

My commitment to a year of outdoor solitude nearly over, I remember beginnings. I was supposed to interrupt my daily routine and trust that my kids wouldn't rearrange the furniture while I was gone. I should expect something from one old pine, acrobat squirrels, black and white wasps that look like a cross between zebras and the Hindenburg.

January is an inhospitable month to begin such a daily sojourn; so be it. I took the sled, my tea, a red woolen cap and dark green coat, and sat. My legs burned from the cold. I gazed and zoned. What could possibly happen here to make it worth shivering for a good three months?

Slowly winter gave over to spring, then spring to summer. By November, I'd seen more than my share of mourning doves sitting on the roof, catbirds wagging their saucy grey tails, mosquitoes rising and falling like chaff against golden light. I'd been greeted by morning mist, frightened by crackling in the darkness, awed by the simplicity of crimson thorn berries. I'd come to think of this place as God's home.

In this home, all things are present. Needles, fallen, silently molder as day fades. Leaves of maple so lately yellow, now disintegrate. Purple asters, white with feathery seed, lose their supple bend and sway. But hemlocks dance in the sharp breeze, evergreen. Wood-winged bushes reach, half-dressed in peach and yellow tongues of fire, Spirit licked. The dog next door is filled with zeal, barking at noisy birds.

The year now fading, I come and remember...the passing of seasons, sorrow and joy, death and life. *Thanksgiving comes soon,* I think. And then, *let my home be as Yours.*

~

"You're a good Mommy," Sonia says in the dark. She touches the side of my face, cradling me with her soft child-fingers. There is something about night that makes her pensive. She pulls me close, kisses my face, tells me she loves me. Sometimes, on a day that hasn't been so good, she complains that I could have done such-and-such and this would have made everything a whole lot better. Night after night we go through these rituals, sometimes joyful, sometimes cranky. Our home is home enough to contain it all for her. She is not afraid to wake up and find that home has disappeared.

My life was different, as I grew up in a situation that severed bonds between my mom and dad, producing two "homes," neither of which could really be considered home. This was no fault of my parents, who provided what I needed in terms of a place to lay my head and gave me very real love. It's just that, as Marquardt notes, when a home splits it doesn't create a sense of two new secure homes, but rather leaves a child feeling there is no home at all. Odd fears crop up, like the anxiety that our important things could disappear at any moment—toys and other valued items.

And indeed, in my experience, they disappeared. Maybe it seems silly to recall how distressed I was when my room got painted dark magenta in my absence (I hated pink and loved the kind of blue that made me think of the sky). Or perhaps it seems odd to bring up how upsetting it felt to come home to a living room that had been rearranged. But these things were unsettling, and over the years, whenever I've been under stress, I've had recurring nightmares that focus on the disappearance of my things or the rearrangement of my environment. Even as recently as the year I spent outdoors, I remember crying out in the night over a dream in which someone came and cut down the pine and the whole hemlock hedge.

Any wonder that I sometimes resist change? My spouse scratches his head in befuddlement. Why can't I see that Grandma's old chair with the horsehair stuffing sticking out and the peeling black and red paint is just that... an old, unattractive chair? Why must I hold so tightly to things, engineer my world, and sometimes seem inhospitable regarding the needs and opinions of others?

---

1. And you?

In your journal, or during a small-group sharing time, complete the thoughts:

"My growing up years gave me (did not give me) a strong sense of home, because..."
"I can relate (cannot relate) to the fear of losing things identified with home, and this makes me feel..."
"I am resistant (not resistant) to change, which has the effect of..."

Marquardt notes that children of divorced families develop a constant disposition of "watching." She says, "In that one place in the world in which any of us should be able to let down our guard—our home— children of divorce have to keep their magnifying glasses up and their thinking caps on... even benign, everyday decisions—'Should I answer the phone? What should I do with the leftovers?' become fraught with tension and moral drama." The sane response would be to scale back on variables. In other words, it's so much easier to make decisions in isolation, to reduce at least one source of tension.

I like to think I'm a pretty sane person. Which could explain my penchant for reducing variables; it hasn't always been easy for me to roll with things and welcome other opinions. Once, one of my overnight guests had a dream. It was raining in the house, she said, and she had ideas about what to do. But I was going 'round ordering everyone to put on green pajamas.

In his book *Setting the Table*, restauranteur Danny Meyer says a successful business will practice the art of *hospitality*, which is different than *service* (or telling people to put on green pj's). "Service is a monologue—how we want to do things and set our own standards... Hospitality, on the other hand, is a dialogue. To be on the guest's side requires listening to that person with every sense and following up with a thoughtful, gracious, appropriate response." One must move from fear to trust, in order to slough off tyranny, ruling, telling, and closed-mindedness and offer collaboration, giving, listening and an openness to learning.

In the end, says Meyer, a hospitable context is a context that makes a guest feel, "This is the place that most makes me feel I've come home." What is the nature of home? Partly, it's a place where we feel we have something in common with people—in other words, where we experience *communion*.

---

2. And you?

In your journal, or during a small-group sharing time, complete the thoughts:

"I prefer to make decisions on my own (with others), because..."
"I can (cannot) see the difference between service and hospitality, as evidenced by..."
"I would describe a hospitable context as..."

I like how the ancient biblical festivals build a communion-based hospitality into their structures—especially the trilogy of harvest festivals, which invite everything to the table: suffering, triumph, sorrow, joy, struggle, comfort, ugliness, beauty, emptiness, plenty, separation, community, death, and life.

The trilogy begins with Passover, which coincides with the barley harvest. It commemorates the night God struck down the firstborn in Egypt, except in households that painted blood on the doorposts as a sign that they should be passed over. Though this meant life for some, the festival is fairly dark in its celebratory elements: flatbread, a slaughtered lamb, and additional items like bitter herbs and parsley dipped in salt water.

Seven weeks later in the Jewish calendar, the tone changes considerably, with the coming of the Feast of Weeks, or Shavuot, which Christians will recognize as Pentecost. The wheat harvest had begun. Flatbread gave over to fat loaves, waved before the Lord. Farmers who had tied ribbons on branches budding with first fruits now harvested these fruits and began a march toward Jerusalem. They sang, danced, trailed behind flute players, and carried baskets of beautiful fruits towards the temple. At the temple, this rowdy crowd was greeted with priestly song — the Levites welcoming pilgrims and accepting the sacrifice of first fruits.

The deliverance that began with Passover was more fully experienced in Shavuot, as the fruits of freedom were recognized and shared. This was no Bacchanal celebration where people simply got drunk on new wine (remember the accusation against the apostles at Pentecost?) and stuffed themselves without regard for the Source of their gifts. Rather, the farmers received in one hand while releasing with the other — a full-circle picture of gratitude and thanks.

Finally, this trilogy of living Psalms ended with Sukkot, the Festival of Booths, which coincided with the fruit harvest. People built booths, and they slept and ate in them. These temporary structures called to mind the wandering of homeless, escaped Israelite slaves in the desert, where they depended fully on God for their sustenance in an unstable life of struggle and impermanence. Although Sukkot commemorated a fragile time, its emphasis was on rejoicing.

In modern versions of Sukkot, celebrants bind together three special items: palm branches, myrtle, and willow. They wave these in all directions to show that God's goodness exists everywhere and recite a blessing. At the same time, they hold what looks like a lemon in their left hand. The elements are aromatic reminders of life. The deliverance that began with Passover blooms in Sukkot. Beauty and abundance attend the command to rejoice. Booths are decorated festively. People, separated from an oppressive past, extend hospitality.

As I suggested before, a startling quality of these festivals is how they invite everything to the table: suffering, triumph, sorrow, joy, struggle, comfort, ugliness, beauty, emptiness, plenty, separation, community, death, and life. All parts of human experience are welcomed and extended love.

When I started feeling more like God's Beloved throughout my year of daily solitude, existence seemed to become a kind of festival, welcoming all manner of emotions, the light and the heavy. Strange things started to happen. I found myself feeling more connected to people and less interested in giving green-pajama advice. I began to want to know strangers' names—I bought a silver bracelet one day and had to know that Tonya had sold it to me; it was important that Jose was my driver to the airport. I had the urge to embrace people and forgive things.

I also began to have unusual responses to events that, in the past, would have elicited far less compassion in me. I'll not soon forget the conversation I had with a new friend, telling her how much I disliked taking care of sick people, how angry it made me, and how little empathy I had. About a week later, she tested the veracity of my claims by unexpectedly throwing up in my bathroom. The test was pretty extensive. I gave her a few moments then grabbed a washcloth from the closet. With cool water, I wiped her face over and again, my heart just about breaking. Next day I called to say, "You're not going to believe this, but all I could think as I washed your face was how very, very lovely you are."

This is not an invitation for the sick people of the world to show up on my doorstep and test my hospitality. Goodness knows, I still have my compassionless days. But the experience was quite profound.

Calhoun says that to practice hospitality we should "treat each guest as though he or she were an angel in disguise," but somehow it had begun to feel different for me. These people all around weren't angels in disguise; they were simply angels. If I can hold this thought for a good long while, I'm thinking I'll continue to develop hospitality not as a prescriptive set of recipes and decorating ideas but as a welcoming state of mind.

---

3. And you?

In your journal, or during a small-group sharing time, complete the thoughts:

"I can see (cannot see) how the biblical festivals welcome all of human experience, in that..."
"I feel (do not feel) connected to people, because..."
"I feel (do not feel) loved by God, and this seems to..."

~

It is winter. Wood-winged bushes are little crosses against the dark yet peachy sky. Crosses upon crosses upon crosses. I say aloud, "I am SO not you, sacrificing for the ones who crossed you," then turn over and put my tongue in the snow. Four licks. I flip back over, sit up, stand. The licks have made a little flame shape. And when I lift the sled, there is no snow angel. Just a sort of wedge.

It seems so long ago, this memory, before I found myself and glimpsed our loving God, in his home beneath the pine.

Playing towards God & discovery

Hospitality partly flows from receptivity, which is rooted in perceiving the "interconnectedness of God and life," notes Nanette Sawyer. In an effort to wake to God's presence in her daily life, then, she plays with musings, asking, "Is God the Force in the wind? Is God the Green in the leaves of the tree just a few feet from my window seat? Is God the Life in the rain pouring into the thirsty roots of all the plants and trees?" She ends by saying, "The idea that God is life, the Life of the life of all living things, [is] a key to the practice of hospitality..."

In the spirit of Sawyer's questions, take a few moments to ask your own questions. Begin with a simple jotting of the objects and people around you. For instance, at this very moment, my list (not exhaustive by any means) might look like this: piano with the top down, radiator, daughter in the kitchen, sound of running water, daughter interrupting as I type this (to show me a painting), daughter interrupting again to ask a question, empty bowl with dirty spoon in it, upside-down bible, French dictionary, a book on poetry as spiritual practice, cello, guitar, green tea, birdsong coming from the little woods, an unruly stack of books on the floor.

Choose just one of the images and make a second list, focused particularly on the item's attributes. For example, I might choose "radiator" and list: cold, cast iron, in the corner, still, rigid, in shadow, ivory-painted, 1930's, molded circle designs, silent, shut down for the season. Next, try writing a quick poem or vignette, beginning with the question, "God are you in [the closed piano, empty bowl... whatever combination of images captures your imagination]? Mine might sound like, "God, are you in the ivory stillness, pressed circles of cold iron, silent corner, shut-down season, shadows? Have you been rooted to this wooden floor since 1930, waiting, just... waiting?" This isn't about writing the perfect piece. It's about playing with words and thoughts to open yourself to the presence and possibility of God and others.

2. A "posture of welcome" or reverence is another step in the hospitality process. Says Sawyer, "In a state of reverence, we stand in the full presence of another, while being fully present ourselves. There is deep acceptance and love in this state, as we encounter the image of God in each other."

Choose a moment to play with feelings of presence and acceptance. Maybe there is a family member you have not been terribly present to this week. Look for an opportunity to engage all your senses with this person. (If you don't feel too odd, it might even be worth trying this with an object. Who knows what you could learn from the cactus in the corner? Or from broken bread at your church's communion table?) Gaze into his/her eyes, feel the special curve of his/her hands, bury your face in his/her hair and get lost in the unique fragrance, listen closely to the sounds of his/her breathing or voice or little habits (my husband, for instance, loves to pace the floor... could I listen intently to his footsteps?); if it's appropriate, kiss the person and note his/her unique flavor. Simply take note without judging. If you feel inspired, write about the experience. Or just tell the person what you discovered and take the opportunity to praise him/her. It is possible that after attending to the other person this way, you might feel distressed instead of joyfully connected. That's okay too. Take it in, wonder.

3. "The completion of the circle of hospitality is generosity. Generosity is a posture of nurture," says Sawyer. Nurture comes in so many forms. It can be the process of planting a seed (literally or figuratively), giving physical or emotional sustenance, picking up the pieces when something has broken (a life, the loss of a life). True nurture flows from receptivity and reverence. There's a fine line between this and duty. For example, when my new friend got sick in my bathroom, you could say it was my duty to clean up. What made it an act of nurture, however, was the love and awe I felt in that moment. Every day, we perform duties, to keep our promises and commitments. And it's okay if those acts don't always burst from a hospitable place. Still, if most of life feels like duty, we might question what's going on.

Sometimes it's hard to pinpoint where we're at. Are we feeling hospitable and offering true nurture? Or are we just moving from duty to duty without much awe? If our life is mostly duty, how did it come to be that way? What can we do to turn things around? Maybe we can find some answers in making noise.

Here's something to try: you probably keep a daily "to do" list in any given week. Dig one out, or a whole week's worth (if you like, add in other events that weren't on the list) and respond musically with the instrument of your choice: your daughter's cello, a toy drum or xylophone (ours is a crocodile!), spoons tapped on a window or counter. You don't need to be a musician to do this. For each item on your list, play out your feelings. (Might you break the window out of frustration over too many items on the list? That's an important discovery.) Don't worry about what to do with your discoveries. Simply listen to what your sounds are telling you and offer them as an expression of the truth to God.

Week 12 prayer

Jesus, you make your home with us and invite us to bring all-that-we-are to the table. Teach me to make my home with others and accept what they bring to the table.

Sabbath on the page

At least several times this week (or every day if you can swing it), try resting on the page by engaging in stream-of-consciousness writing. Do this for at least several pages. Feel free to bring all-that-you-are to the page, as kind of openness to God.

Blog it, to process and share

It's the end of week twelve. Consider blogging about your experience. If you don't blog, you can do a "week-in-review" in your journal or write a letter to a friend or God. You could include:

• An idea that was new to you, or a quote you appreciated
• Something you liked about your experience
• Something you felt anxious or unsure about
• Any questions you have (no need to answer them; sometimes the asking is the most important step)
• Things you were reminded of: a story, memory, piece of art or music, bible verse or prayer, poem, current or historical event

Epilogue

It is my practice to clean the little woods. I pick up sticks, prune branches, trim ivy. Sometimes I find a blue Frisbee that has made its way over the fence, or a yellow football, and I toss them back. Once, I found red yarn in an oak sapling. Another time I discovered the missing plastic container my daughter used to make a squirrel-proof birdfeeder (he was greatly offended, it seemed, so stole the whole contraption and hid it in the prickly pines). One day I mentioned my cleaning practice to our eldest daughter. She laughed, "You can't clean up the woods."

~

I'm not sure what I expected from a year of solitude in our little woods and an exploration of spiritual practices. Changes, I guess. Discoveries. I feel compelled to reveal, "this is what I learned," but I also feel inadequate for the task.

As an act of communion, it seems appropriate to borrow words, poetic words from my twelve-year-old daughter Sara. She too has loved a wooded place; it borders the property of our church. For five years she played there each week, with a certain set of friends. Next year the woods will still be there, but the friends won't be. She used this situation to partly answer a question put to her by a teacher, "What's the most important thing you learned this year?" This is what she said...

*I learned that sometimes there isn't one answer I can
think of for this question. And I learned that Michaela
and Noah and Eli are not coming back next year (and
the rest will never come), and I learned that someday*

*I might want to go across the log and I learned that
you can't sun-cook with aluminum foil and an empty*

orange juice bottle, wild mustard leaves, in the woods
and I learned that I keep trying to write about the

woods and I can't and I know even if we can go back
there with them it won't be the same. And I learned
that gardens and bridges and water catchers for plants
and building ziplines don't actually work or happen but

we do them anyway and I don't know why. Well, I do
actually, sort of. We do it because it's something to
do, but after we knew they weren't coming back it was
as if we were trying to do everything before it was gone

and I learned to teach cello and write villanelles and I
learned that sometimes answers are right in front of
you already and you just have to find them and I
learned that there are some things you can't stop...

even if you really, really want to.

These words say things I need to say. They tell us it is an impossible task to try to express, "this is what I learned." And yet, the lines ache with revelation. She learned she couldn't sun-cook with aluminum foil, just as I learned I couldn't really practice certain things like gratitude and presence. She learned that water catchers and ziplines don't work or happen, but she and her friends tried them anyway, just as I learned that spiritual practices are one part dream and one part grounding reality.

My daughter learned that five years together were both a beginning and an end... someday she may yet cross that log, but her friends won't be coming with her. In the same way, I discovered that my practices had promise and limitation; someday they may help me be new things I want to be, but I won't ever clean up all the frailties within. Or maybe

I'll change certain personal rhythms, move on, while friends or family go their separate ways. Spiritual practices strive for communion, but they can also divide.

She learned that answers are often right in front of you. You needn't necessarily go far to find what you need. To this, I think of something Sittser said, "... some people embarked on pilgrimage to major religious centers, most often to perform some kind of penance, to pray for a miracle, to recover from some catastrophic loss or to visit places renowned for their holiness... the wealthy and powerful often embarked on long pilgrimages, to famous, faraway places. Common people had to be content staying closer to home." I'm thinking my back yard counts as staying closer to home. And I can say I found some answers, healing and small miracles, a few steps from my door.

I like how my daughter celebrates her successes. Teaching cello, writing villanelles. She is far from being a musical virtuoso, but she was able to pass on knowledge to another person who knew less than she. Her villanelles aren't perfect models of the form, but they are lovely and thoughtful. Likewise, I've come to understand that spiritual practice is just that... practice, or perhaps more accurately it is simply the act of participation. It is not control. It is not perfection. And I don't have to wait until I ascend to some magical place to share my discoveries with others.

My daughter is also right in saying that you can't stop certain things even if you want to. You can't stop life from moving on. You can't stop pain and failure, past or future. No, you can't stop the sticks from falling, ivy from creeping, squirrels from stealing your homemade birdfeeders; my daughter is right... you can't clean up the little woods. But you can embrace the life you have before it's gone.

Wonder: discussion or reflection questions

In the little woods, I often found myself wondering. What is that white fluff clinging to the undersides of the pine branches? Why is the squirrel staring at me and flicking his tail? What kind of fly is this, so tiny and iridescent crimson? Can my neighbor see me from his garage?

Questions can lead, guide, open or close us. Maybe that's why Jesus and the prophets were fond of asking questions. I offer a few...

Chapter 1 Woods • invitation

1. Is there an area of your life where you feel "pinched" by the boundaries you've either chosen or been given by life circumstance?

2. Are there any commitments that have been inviting you lately? What makes them appealing? Is anything holding you back?

3. It is during mindless drifting that our deepest needs often come to the surface. Do you have quiet spaces, places in your day, to let yourself simply drift? If not, how might you begin to carve out a niche for them?

4. Your mirrors may reflect that you need to change in certain ways (mirrors could be the words and expressions of others, formal evaluations, emotions such as anger or depression). What are they saying? Do the things your mirrors reflect coincide with your own sense of need for growth or change? If not, what do you make of this?

5. Are there dark places in your soul you'd rather hide? That's natural, and no one is going to try to drag these things out of you in confession. But if you could express the dark places as a particular hunger, what would you say you are hungry for?

6. What are the conditions you regularly make space for, to promote your spiritual transformation? Think carefully... there may be some you overlook because they don't seem overtly spiritual. Are you fairly satisfied with the conditions you create to promote transformation?

7. In what way is creation/transformation always "a partnership" for healing?

Chapter 2 Rules • the way

1. Whose job is it to keep your life from "falling into nothing"? Yours or God's? Depending on your answer, is this how you actually function on a practical level?

2. Are there ways in which you feel it's time to "learn to fly"? What either urges or holds you back from leaving your familiar nest to try? If you already feel that you're on the ground, what might guide, protect, and assist you in the process of learning?

3. Have you ever had an experience when it felt like the Holy Spirit was "wheeling and screaming", urging you to learn fly? How did you sense the Spirit's presence and intentions?

4. Do you encourage your "mirrors" to reflect the truth of you to you? What aspects of your personality and behavior might discourage them from reflecting such truth?

5. What kinds of spiritual practices does your particular community emphasize? Consider how this is both helpful and possibly limiting.

6. You can't do it all—sixty-five spiritual practices and counting. Are there practices that stand out to you as being particularly important for

the kinds of growth you currently need? One way to consider this question is to skim Calhoun's *Spiritual Disciplines Handbook* and consult the Appendices in Barton's *Sacred Rhythms*.

Chapter 3: Look • contemplation

1. Contemplation can mean "marking out a temple." In what ways does this phrase either encapsulate or oppose your understanding of contemplation?

2. Leonardo DaVinci noted that marvelous ideas arise from indistinct things; he'd as soon look at stains on walls, as he would stained-glass windows. His approach was contemplative, in the sense that it had an "all-embracing quality." What kinds of conditions might help promote a similar all-embracing quality to your spiritual observations?

3. The question arises, what to contemplate? Have you been taught a hierarchy of acceptable subjects for contemplation? Do certain areas like art, nature, or music seem too off-the-map in their possibilities for revealing God and transforming your inner life? Whether your answer is yes or no, explore your reasons for thinking the way you do.

4. How do you think engaging in contemplation might help you develop patience (or not)?

5. Think about these questions from Comins, "Do we find God in printed words, through reading learned texts and praying the inherited words of the prayer book? Or do we find God at the original site of revelation, in the natural world, without words at all? ... Do I recite a psalm praising the Creator for the grandeur of nature, or do I just look up?"

6. Do you think it is too self-focused to contemplate your personal his-

tory and present landscape, as part of your spiritual practice? Why or why not.

Chapter 4: Weep • celebration

1. Celebration does not occur in a vacuum, but rather in temples of time and space. What kinds of predictable celebrations are currently a part of your life? How do they change from month-to-month or year-to-year, and how do they stay the same?

2. Did your childhood offer a predictable set of structures, spiritual or otherwise, through which you learned to celebrate life? Describe your memories.

3. Would you describe yourself as more of a closed or open person? What dynamics have shaped you to be so? Are you satisfied with how you are?

4. Do you seem to have a capacity for joy, or does your emotional body feel like it's shrunken to a "bland middle"? Consider what kinds of contexts promote more of a range of feeling in you. Are they "spiritual" contexts, or something else?

5. Sometimes the only way out is in. Are there particular griefs you might need to explore and embrace more deeply, in order to increase your capacity for joy and love?

6. What do you think about the idea that predictable celebrations can heal the wounds of dysfunction? (These can be personal celebrations you dream up, celebrations based on the church calendar, or borrowed festivals from our sister-faith Judaism.) Are there new celebrations you'd like to try, as a way to heal broken places, promote your growth?

Chapter 5: Sky • gratitude

1. Religious architecture through the ages left "holes" in the ceilings of sacred buildings, as an invitation for spiritual exchange. Consider the architecture of your life. Where have you set up dependable shelters with openings to the Divine?

2. Do you feel like a person who has gratitude? Do the observations and reactions of others seem to parallel this sense you have of yourself?

3. What do you think produces gratitude in your life? And, conversely, what does gratitude produce?

4. Are there losses in your life that have caused you to be overly self-protective? Are you able to step out and dream, or does fear of further loss hold you back? Consider that however we operate in life can spill over into our relationship with God.

5. Lewis Hyde says, "Between the time a gift comes to us and the time we pass it along, we suffer gratitude." If we do not suffer gratitude upon receiving a gift, what might be the cause?

6. Describe a moment when you've felt pure gratitude. What were the circumstances? Do you think you can orchestrate such gratitude? Is there any reason to try to do so?

Chapter 6: Open • prayer

1. What is the nature and purpose of spiritual practice? Is it straightforward for you, like the idea of studying to prepare for a test? Or does it seem to be more art than formula? Which way of looking at spiritual practice resonates with the current needs of your life?

2. Do you struggle with either the tendency to fight others or flee them during conflict? In what ways can both fighting and fleeing be healthy responses? In what ways can they hold you back from connecting to others and experiencing personal peace?

3. How do either fight or flight responses potentially affect the need in prayer to "offer our bodies and souls to God in trust and passionate hope" like the woman in *Song of Songs*?

4. Now switch gears. Are you comfortable with thinking of God as occupying a similar role to that of the woman in *Song of Songs*? Why or why not?

5. In what ways is your approach to God sometimes like a crass approach and exit?

6. How do you feel about the idea that prayer can simply be a "wordless, inchoate unhappiness"? Or that just showing up to the same place every day and allowing yourself to think bare and raw before God could be a kind of prayer?

Chapter 7: Gone • Presence

1. Levitical law suggested separation between a woman and man during her period (I say *suggested*, because there's room for interpretation, depending on the passage consulted). Can you see this suggestion as a form of grace? Since this law was grouped with additional laws about "uncleanness," it's easy to overlook other possible ways of understanding the law.

2. How do you react to times of separation in your life... separation from loved-ones, work, or technology?

3. Perhaps you are in midlife; perhaps not. What kinds of pressures have added up in your own life as you've aged? Do you feel you are handling them in healthy ways?

4. When pressures build up and you begin to weaken, what areas of your life tend to be most vulnerable first? (relationships, work responsibilities, physical well-being?) Mini-breakdowns in vulnerable areas of your life can be your life's attempt at forced separation and rest; consider how you might listen to your mini-breakdowns as a kind of red flag that something needs to give.

5. Do you believe that departure and separation contribute to a greater sense of presence? How have you experienced this in relationship to God and others, in the workplace or physically?

6. Is there an area in your life—whether church, home, or work—where you have been finding it hard to separate at times? How has this affected you and the various communities you are a part of? Do these communities support or work against times of separation?

Chapter 8: Cycle • Sabbath

1. Do you tend to be a person who goes and goes, taking little predictable time for rest and celebration? Are you satisfied with this kind of life? If you are a person who does take predictable time for rest and celebration, what has helped you develop a capacity for rhythmic living?

2. Do any of the following characteristics describe you: fear cycles of presence and absence...act strong, refuse rest, work extra hard, eschew play. If you don't approach life in this manner, share the dynamics you think enable you to be otherwise.

3. Has your life—church or devotional life included—gone beyond healthy productivity to bondage because you lack built-in rhythms of rest and play?

4. "To pause is to trust." If you have difficulty building in times of pause from people, work, or technology, what is the source of that difficulty?

5. In what ways is Sabbath an "invitation to go nowhere"? Is that how you experience Sabbath in your life?

6. How might Sabbath allow us to try on different aspects of life? Do you feel comfortable in thinking God instituted the Sabbath partly for this reason? What other reasons, perhaps not recognizably "spiritual" might God have had for instituting the Sabbath? If you practice Sabbath, share how this has played out in reality; if you don't practice Sabbath, consider trying it out for at least a month, to see how it promises to alter your life.

Chapter 9: Poetry • silence

1. When was the last time you sat in silence? What did it feel like to do so? If you can't remember a recent experience in silence, what dynamics have kept you in the presence of noise?

2. How does the experience of silence feel to you: punishing or nurturing? Do you ever feel the presence of God in silence?

3. "Listening is the path to intimacy," says poet John Fox. Do you agree?

4. Even if you have no interest in writing poetry, the experience of using it as a listening tool can be helpful. Choose an object or a person to really listen to right now. What is it "saying" to you? Jot this down in lines.

Do you believe that such listening could have anything to do with your relationship to God?

5. The poetic Psalms provide a home for our confusion, a healing place for our disillusionment, a place to breathe. What is it about poetry that can make this possible, in a way that prose sometimes cannot?

6. Do any active approaches to silence appeal to you? Writing, drawing, walking alone, something else? Do you believe that God can show up in silence, regardless of the type of silence you choose to immerse yourself in? If yes, try to remember a specific experience to illustrate.

Chapter 10: Me • self care

1. Think about the nature of your relationships. Do you tend to take the blame for failures on yourself? Or do you always push the blame in the direction of the other person? In what way might these two responses actually be similar?

2 Do you think you love yourself? If not or if so, how might this affect your relationship to God and others?

3. Have you ever seen your soul "as queen" and not just beggar? What kinds of experiences contributed to that sense? If you've only seen your soul as beggar, what kinds of background experiences have led you to that kind of vision.

4. Calhoun asserts, "the fact that the Holy Spirit wants to abide in us is one way we know how infinitely precious and beloved we are." If you are infinitely precious and beloved, how does this suggest you should treat yourself on a practical level?

5. If you are the kind of person who lays down your life for others, do you do it out of love or an inner despair regarding your worth? What would a godly laying-down-of life look like, in your opinion?

6. In what ways, if any, do you act as a frequent bridge person? Consider various contexts: work, home, church, community. Has this led to undue stress in your life? How does this ultimately fit or not fit with a godly existence?

Chapter 11: With • submission

1. Can caretaking be a form of submission? When might it not be?

2. Have you ever spent time with a "caretaker" type person? Describe the experience.

3. Do you believe it's possible for submission to have different faces— giving versus receiving, leading versus following?

4. Respond to the suggestion that submission could be framed as "the art of working with."

5. Do you think Jesus was the submissive or non-submissive type? Try to think of contrasting examples. Is there a thread that might bind these contrasts together?

6. If you were to practice submission, what kinds of things might you do the same as you currently do. Differently?

Chapter 12: Home • hospitality

1. Are you a fairly flexible person, or do you tend more towards watch-

fulness, control and resistance to change? How does this affect your relationship to others?

2. When dealing with others do you tend to be more service or hospitality oriented? Service is "a monologue—how we want to do things and set our own standards", while hospitality is "a dialogue [that] requires listening to [others] with every sense and following up with a thoughtful, gracious response."

3. When you think about your "home" and compare it to the Jewish trilogy of harvest festivals, how is it similar or different? Do you welcome the whole range of human experience* as you interact with people? (*suffering, triumph, sorrow, joy, struggle, comfort, ugliness, beauty, emptiness, plenty, separation, community, death and life) Why or why not?

4. Do you feel beloved by God? Do you feel a keen sense of connection to other people? Explain.

5. Describe the internal responses you have when caring for others, in joyful or difficult circumstances.

6. How have you tended to define hospitality? More as a prescriptive set of behaviors or a welcoming state of mind? Would it make any difference to think one way versus the other? Consider the hospitality of God. Does either definition seem more descriptive of his character and practice? Or do both apply?

Endnotes

Week 1: Woods • Invitation

page 1   "Without knowledge of the self": John Calvin, "The Institutes," quoted by Adele Calhoun in *Spiritual Disciplines Handbook: Practices that Transform Us* (Downers Grove, Ill: InterVarsity Press, 2005), p. 23.

page 2   "For those fields hold their soil": Wendell Berry, *The Gift of Good Land: Further Essays Cultural and Agricultural* (San Francisco: North Point Press, 1981), p. 26.

page 3   A book about living with limits: Jim Merkel, *Radical Simplicity: Small Footprints on a Finite Earth* (Gabriola Island, BC, Canada: New Society Publishers, 2003).

page 3   Annie Dillard-style trip to the Galapagos: Annie Dillard, *Teaching a Stone to Talk: Expeditions and Encounters* (New York: Harper Perennial, a division of HarperCollinsPublishers, 1982), p. 108.

page 5   Creative work is "an event and a partnership": Vinita Hampton Wright, *The Soul Tells a Story: Engaging Creativity With Spirituality in the Writing Life* (Downers Grove, Ill: InterVarsity Press, 2005), p. 64.

page 5   "Think of it this way": Ibid, p.126.

page 7   The youngest child asks four questions: Rachel Musleah, *Why on This Night? A Passover Haggadah for Family Cel-*

ebration (New York: Simon and Schuster, 2000), p. 46.

page 7 "To restore the soul is to renew the healthy": Kent Ira Groff, *Writing Tides: Finding Grace and Growth Through Writing* (Nashville, TN: Abingdon Press, 2007), p. 44.

Week 2: Rules • The Way

page 11 "In the end, this is the most hopeful thing": Ruth Haley Barton, *Sacred Rhythms: Arranging Our Lives for Spiritual Transformation* (Downers Grove, Ill: InterVarsity Press, 2006), p. 12.

page 12 "He showed me something small, no bigger than a hazel-nut": Julian of Norwich, *Showings*, translated from the critical text by Edmund Colledge, OSA and James Walsh, SJ, preface by Jean Leclercq, OSB. (New York: Paulist Press, 1978), p. 183.

page 15 We can become like Christ: Dallas Willard, *The Spirit of the Disciplines: Understanding How God Changes Lives* (New York: HarperOne, 1990), p. ix.

page 15 "We search for stated ways and methods of learning how to love God": Brother Lawrence, foreward by Mother Tessa Bielecki, *The Practice of the Presence of God, With Spiritual Maxims* (Boston: New Seeds, 2005), p. xi.

page 18 "To live as a farmer, one has to come": Wendell Berry, *The Way of Ignorance and Other Essays* (New York: Shoemaker and Hoard, an imprint of Avalon Publishing Group, Inc., 2005), p. 46.

Week 3: Look • Contemplation

page 21   "Looking is the beginning of seeing": Corita Kent in
           Corita Kent and Jan Steward, *Learning by Heart: Teach-
           ings to Free the Creative Spirit* (New York: Allworth Press,
           2008), p. 33.

page 21   "The Contemplative was a person who undertook": Ira
           Progoff, *The Cloud of Unknowing: A New Translation of a
           Classic Guide to Spiritual Experience Revealing the Dy-
           namics of the Inner Life From a Particular Historical and
           Religious Point of View* (New York: The Julian Press, Inc.,
           1957), p. 21.

page 22   "Assumes an open, all-embracing": Gerald G. May, MD.,
           *The Dark Night of the Soul: A Psychiatrist Explores the Con-
           nection Between Darkness and Spiritual Growth* (New
           York: HarperSanFrancisco, a division of HarperCollins
           Publishers, 2004), p. 109.

page 22   Contemplation involves gazing, with faith: Adele Cal-
           houn, *Spiritual Disciplines Handbook: Practices that Trans-
           form Us* (Downers Grove, Ill: InterVarsity Press, 2005), p.
           50.

page 22   "Do not despise my opinion when I remind you":
           Leonardo Da Vinci quoted by Richard Restak, M.D., in
           *Mozart's Brain and the Fighter Pilot: Unleashing Your
           Brain's Potential* (New York: Harmony Books, a trademark
           of Random House Inc., 2001), pp. 180-181.

page 24   "Christ doesn't just lord it over": Calvin Miller, *Celtic De-*

votions: a Guide to Morning and Evening Prayer (Downers Grove, Ill: InterVarsity Press, 2008), p. 37.

page 24 "I thought about the great debate..." Rabbi Mike Comins, *A Wild Faith: Jewish Ways into Wilderness, Wilderness Ways into Judaism* (Woodstock, VT: Jewish Lights Publishing, 2007), p. 4.

page 26 "Not through effort but through darkness" Gerald L. Sittser, *Water from a Deep Well: Christian Spirituality from Early Martyrs to Modern Missionaries* (Downers Grove, Ill: InterVarsity Press, 2007), p. 184.

page 26 "Untethered, floating above the realities of our embodied lives": Parker Palmer quoted in Gerald G. May, *The Wisdom of Wilderness: Experiencing the Healing Power of Nature* (New York: HarperCollinsPublishers, 2006), p. xii.

page 27 Child experiences divorce as a "sudden death" which creates an "overwhelming internal panic": Judith Wallerstein, Julia M. Lewis and Sandra Blakeslee, *The Unexpected Legacy of Divorce: A 25-Year Landmark Study* (New York: Hyperion, 2000), p. 27.

page 27 Alcoholics can't give us what we need: Melody Beattie, *Codependent No More: How to Stop Controlling Others and Start Caring for Yourself* (Deerfield Beach, Florida: Hazelden, 1986) pp. 94-95.

page 28 "Centeredness in the present moment": Gerald G. May, MD., *The Dark Night of the Soul: A Psychiatrist Explores the Connection Between Darkness and Spiritual Growth*

(New York: HarperSanFrancisco, a division of Harper-CollinsPublishers, 2004), p. 109.

Week 4: Weep • Celebration

page 31   "We spend too little time experiencing the griefs": David Whyte, *The Heart Aroused: Poetry and the Preservation of the Soul in Corporate America* (New York: Doubleday. A division of Random House, 2002), p. 105.

page 32   Practice celebration by doing what makes us feel joyful: Adele Calhoun, *Spiritual Disciplines Handbook: Practices that Transform Us* (Downers Grove, Ill: InterVarsity Press, 2005), p. 26.

page 32   Choose a context: Ibid, p. 28.

page 33   Child experiences divorce as a "sudden death" which "permanently alters a child's life" and "represents the end of childhood": Judith Wallerstein, Julia M. Lewis and Sandra Blakeslee, *The Unexpected Legacy of Divorce: A 25-Year Landmark Study* (New York: Hyperion, 2000), p. 27.

page 33   "The parents' interaction was a black hole": Ibid, p. 34.

page 35   "It is as if the two are simply two": David Whyte, *The Heart Aroused: Poetry and the Preservation of the Soul in Corporate America* (New York: Doubleday. A division of Random House, 2002), pp.105-106.

page 35   People who live with alcoholics often refuse to enjoy life: Melody Beattie, *Codependent No More: How to Stop Con-*

trolling Others and Start Caring for Yourself (Deerfield Beach, Florida: Hazelden, 1986), p. 111.

page 36   "Unconsciously refuse to grow any older" in that part of us that's been traumatized "until that trauma is resolved": David Whyte, *The Heart Aroused: Poetry and the Preservation of the Soul in Corporate America* (New York: Doubleday. A division of Random House, 2002), p. 125.

page 37   Ritual-making can help us deal with the important phases: Gertrude Nelson, *To Dance With God: Family Ritual and Community Celebration* (New York: Paulist Press, 1986), p. 24.

page 38   "We are overawed by our ritual habits: Ibid, p. 12.

page 38   Some basic elements Nelson suggests we include: Ibid, pp. 51-52.

Week 5: Sky • Gratitude

page 41   "Between the time a gift comes to us": Lewis Hyde, *The Gift: Creativity and the Artist in the Modern World* (New York: Vintage, an imprint of Alfred A. Knopf, 2007), p. 60.

page 41   Religious architecture made allowance: Gertrude Nelson, *To Dance With God: Family Ritual and Community Celebration* (New York: Paulist Press, 1986), p. 27.

page 42   "A holy space, set aside, that also works as a shelter": Ibid, p. 28.

page 43   Gratitude can free us: Adele Calhoun, *Spiritual Disciplines Handbook: Practices that Transform Us* (Downers Grove, Ill: InterVarsity Press, 2005), p. 29.

page 43   If memories were sparrows poem: Anonymous commenter at *Seedlings in Stone* (January 28, 2009) <https://www.blogger.com/comment.g?blogID=31909451&postID=1392114363314222402>

page 44   Oppressive rules quell the open expression of feelings: Melody Beattie, *Codependent No More: How to Stop Controlling Others and Start Caring for Yourself* (Deerfield Beach, Florida: Hazelden, 1986), p. 28.

page 45   Where a child learns to step lightly, put on a good face: Elizabeth Marquardt, *Between Two Worlds: the Inner Lives of Children of Divorce* (New York: Crown Publishers, an imprint of the Crown Publishing Group, a division of Random House, Inc., 2005), p. 124.

page 46   "In endless space, we create a fixed point": Gertrude Nelson, *To Dance With God: Family Ritual and Community Celebration* (New York: Paulist Press, 1986), pp. 25-26.

page 48   "With gifts that are agents of change": Lewis Hyde, *The Gift: Creativity and the Artist in the Modern World* (New York: Vintage, an imprint of Alfred A. Knopf, 2007), p. 60.

Week 6: Open • Prayer

page 51   "See? This is who I am": Gerald May, *Addiction and Grace:*

Love and Spirituality in the Healing of Addictions (New York: HarperOne, 2007), p. 168.

page 53   Family dysfunction teaches us things: Murphy Toerner, *Murphy's Devotions blog* (March 24, 2009) <http://mur physdevotions.blogspot.com/>.

page 54   "Jesus is totally folded in on Himself": Sister Wendy Beckett, *Sister Wendy on Prayer* (New York: Harmony books, an imprint of Crown Publishing Group, a division of Random House, Inc., 2006), p. 49.

page 54   "The essential act of prayer is to stand unprotected": Ibid, p. 38.

page 56   Definition of *precarious*: Dictionary.com <http://dictio nary.reference.com/browse/precarious>.

page 57   "Exactly what we are, each of us": Ibid, pp. 76-77.

page 58   "Our failure to lament...cuts us off": Michael Card, *A Sacred Sorrow: Reaching Out to God in the Lost Language of Lament* (Colorado Springs, Colorado: NavPress, 2005), p. 29.

page 58   "A clump of bluebonnets": Megan Willome, "Still." Used by permission.

page 59   Our brains cannot keep more than one emotion: Richard Restak, M.D., *Mozart's Brain and the Fighter Pilot: Unleashing Your Brain's Potential* (New York: Harmony Books, a trademark of Random House Inc., 2001), p. 40.

Week 7: Gone • Presence

page 61   "Do that until you ache": Rumi quoted by Daniel
           Ladinksy, *Love Poems from God: Twelve Sacred Voices from
           the East and West* (New York: Penguin Compass, The Pen-
           guin Group, 2002), p. 85.

page 62   Levitical passages on menstruation: 15:19-30; 18:19;
           20:18.

page 63   "It is at the margins that the weaknesses": Wendell Berry,
           *The Gift of Good Land: further Essays Cultural and Agri-
           cultural* (San Francisco: North Point Press, 1981), p. 66.

page 68   "Absence sharpens our seeking": Steven Chase, *The Tree of
           Life: Models of Christian Prayer* (Grand Rapids, Michi-
           gan: Baker Academic, a division of Baker Publishing
           Group, 2005), p. 209.

page 68   Despite all the red lights: Billy Coffey, "Redneck Love,"
           Billy Coffey <http://www.billycoffey.com/2009/06/red
           neck-love/>.

Week 8: Cycle • Sabbath

page 71   "Because it sets its own pace": Lewis Hyde, *The Gift: Cre-
           ativity and the Artist in the Modern World* (New York:
           Vintage, an imprint of Alfred A. Knopf, 2007), p. 64.

page 72   "Family that created [them] simply vanished": Judith
           Wallerstein, Julia M. Lewis and Sandra Blakeslee, *The Un-
           expected Legacy of Divorce: A 25-Year Landmark Study*

(New York: Hyperion, 2000), p. 162.

page 72   When the marriage falls apart, mom generally falls apart too... "unimaginably traumatic...": Ibid, p. 171.

page 74   39 categories of Sabbath prohibitions: Wikipedia.org <http://en.wikipedia.org/wiki/Activities_prohibited_on _Shabbat>.

page 74   Hebrew root for the word "Sabbath" includes "pause": Lynne M. Baab, *Sabbath Keeping: Finding Freedom in the Rhythms of Rest* (Downers Grove IL: InterVarsity Press, 2005), p. 38.

page 79   "Wayne asked how the church was doing": Gordon Atkinson, "Covenant Stories: Lillian's Eyes," at *HighCalling Blogs* <http://highcallingblogs.com/blog/covenant-sto-ries-lillians-eyes/2709/>.

Week 9: Poetry • Silence

page 83   "Deeply listening to what is within and around us changes us": John Fox, *Finding What you Didn't Lose: Expressing Your Truth and Creativity Through Poem-Making* (New York: Tarcher, an imprint of Penguin USA,1995), p. 34.

page 84   "Noise is part of the business ethic": Stuart Simm, "Shhhh" in *The Humanist* <http://newhumanist.org. uk/938>.

page 84   "Stroll...talking into tiny bits of plastic": Lauren F. Winner,

"Against the Cell" in *Boundless* <http://www.boundless. org/2005/articles/a0001207.cfm>.

page 85   "Listening is the path to intimacy," John Fox, *Finding What you Didn't Lose: Expressing Your Truth and Creativity Through Poem-Making* (New York: Tarcher, an imprint of Penguin USA,1995), p. 13.

page 86   Desert saint, to overcome gossip and frivolous talk: Gerald L. Sittser, *Water from a Deep Well: Christian Spirituality from Early Martyrs to Modern Missionaries* (Downers Grove, Ill: InterVarsity Press, 2007), p. 86.

page 86   Make note of movement sounds, voice sounds: John Fox, *Finding What you Didn't Lose: Expressing Your Truth and Creativity Through Poem-Making* (New York: Tarcher, an imprint of Penguin USA,1995), p. 15.

page 87   "I am fizzle": L.L. Barkat, "Bottled," in *InsideOut: Poems* (New York: International Arts Movement, 2009). Used by permission.

page 87   We bring the same patterns of intimacy: Ruth Haley Barton, *Sacred Rhythms: Arranging Our Lives for Spiritual Transformation* (Downers Grove, Ill: InterVarsity Press, 2006), p. 67.

page 88   "Become a world-famous poet...a home for your bewilderment": John Fox, *Finding What you Didn't Lose: Expressing Your Truth and Creativity Through Poem-Making* (New York: Tarcher, an imprint of Penguin USA,1995), pp. 2-3.

page 88   Untitled poem in comment box: Laure Kreuger, *High-CallingBlogs* <http://highcallingblogs.com/blog/poetry-as-spiritual-practice-part-2/2490/#comments>. Used by permission.

page 89   "Arnoldian notion of poetry replacing religion": Christian Wiman, "Gazing into the Abyss," *The Amercian Scholar* (Summer, 2007) <http://www.theamericanscholar.org/gazing-into-the-abyss/>.

page 90   It is different than simple hearing: Dictionary.com <http://dictionary.reference.com/browse/listen>.

page 91   Recommended resource: Mark Strand and Eavan Boland, eds., *The Making of a Poem: The Norton Anthology of Poetic Forms* (New York: W. W. Norton and Company, 2001).

page 91   Recommended resource: Laurance Wieder, *The Poets' Book of Psalms: The Complete Psalter as Rendered by Twenty-Five Poets from the Sixteenth to the Twentieth Centuries* (Oxford University Press USA, 1999).

Week 10: Me • Selfcare

page 93   "There cannot be a stressful crisis": Henry Kissinger quoted at *Stress Relief Tools* <http://www.stress-relief-tools.com/stress-quotes.html>.

page 94   "Why do we not leave home": L.L. Barkat, "Stayed," in *InsideOut: Poems* (New York: International Arts Movement, 2009). Used by permission.

page 95   Achiever, Activator, Arranger: Tom Rath, *StrengthsFinder 2.0* (New York: Gallup Press, 2007).

page 95   Kids serve as bridge: Elizabeth Marquardt, *Between Two Worlds: the Inner Lives of Children of Divorce* (New York: Crown Publishers, an imprint of the Crown Publishing Group, a division of Random House, Inc., 2005), p. 28.

page 96   We don't know our needs, we judge them bad or wrong: Melody Beattie, *Codependent No More: How to Stop Controlling Others and Start Caring for Yourself* (Deerfield Beach, Florida: Hazelden, 1986), p. 165.

page 98   "Now I place my hand upon you": Walt Whitman, "To You," at *Bartelby* <http://www.bartleby.com/142/175.html>.

page 99   "Self-care is never a selfish act": Parker Palmer quoted by Adele Calhoun in *Spiritual Disciplines Handbook: Practices that Transform Us* (Downers Grove, Ill: InterVarsity Press, 2005), p. 71.

page 100   "Moon shines, glassy blue": L.L. Barkat, "Untitled," in *InsideOut: Poems* (New York: International Arts Movement, 2009). Used by permission.

page 100   Calhoun recommends AA: Adele Calhoun, *Spiritual Disciplines Handbook: Practices that Transform Us* (Downers Grove, Ill: InterVarsity Press, 2005), p. 73.

page 101   Stress is more than an unpleasant feeling: John Medina, *Brain Rules: 12 Principles for Surviving and Thriving at*

Work, Home, and School (Seattle, WA: Pear Press, 2009), pp. 176-179.

page 101   Bridge experiment: Carol A. Johmann, *Bridges: Amazing Structures to Design, Build & Test* (Charlotte, VT: Williamson Publishing Company, imprint of Ideals Publications, Inc., 1999), pp. 20-21.

page 102   Resource on making choices: Ruth Haley Barton, *Sacred Rhythms: Arranging Our Lives for Spiritual Transformation* (Downers Grove, Ill: InterVarsity Press, 2006).

page 102   Resource to organize life: Leo Babauta, *The Power of Less: The Fine Art of Limiting Yourself to the Essential... In Business and in Life* (New York: Hyperion, 2008).

Week 11: With • Submission

page 105   "Only strength can cooperate": Dwight D. Eisenhower, quoted at *Brainy Quote* <http://www.brainyquote.com/quotes/quotes/d/dwightdei149092.html>.

page 106   In order to keep from seeming too much like mom: Elizabeth Marquardt, *Between Two Worlds: the Inner Lives of Children of Divorce* (New York: Crown Publishers, an imprint of the Crown Publishing Group, a division of Random House, Inc., 2005), p. 31.

page 106   Dynamics are remarkably similar to the those in the alcoholic household: Melody Beattie, *Codependent No More: How to Stop Controlling Others and Start Caring for Your-*

self (Deerfield Beach, Florida: Hazelden, 1986), pp. 78-79.

page 107   "Letting go, of course, is a scary enterprise": Elizabeth Gilbert, *Eat, Pray, Love: One Woman's Search for Everything Across Italy, India and Indonesia* (New York: Penguin Books/The Penguin Group, 2006), pp. 155-156.

page 108   The confusion Beattie says caretakers often feel: Melody Beattie, *Codependent No More: How to Stop Controlling Others and Start Caring for Yourself* (Deerfield Beach, Florida: Hazelden, 1986), p. 28.

page 108   "Caretaking breeds anger. Caretakers become angry parents": Ibid, p. 86.

page 108   "Sometimes submission means giving": Adele Calhoun, *Spiritual Disciplines Handbook: Practices that Transform Us* (Downers Grove, Ill: InterVarsity Press, 2005), p. 119.

page 109   "Refusal to speak at such a moment": John Leax, *Grace is Where I Live: The Landscape of Faith and Writing* (La Porte, Indiana: Word Farm, 1993, 2004), p. 91.

Week 12: Home • Hospitality

page 115   "Hospitality is a state of mind": Duchess, source unkown.

page 116   Leaves a child feeling there is no home at all: Elizabeth Marquardt, *Between Two Worlds: the Inner Lives of Children of Divorce* (New York: Crown Publishers, an imprint of the Crown Publishing Group, a division of Random

House, Inc., 2005), p. 59.

page 117   "In that one place in the world in which any of us should be able to let down our guard: Elizabeth Marquardt, *Between Two Worlds: the Inner Lives of Children of Divorce* (New York: Crown Publishers, an imprint of the Crown Publishing Group, a division of Random House, Inc., 2005), p. 91.

page 118   "Service is a monologue": Danny Meyer, *Setting the Table: The Transforming Power of Hospitality in Business* (New York: Harper Paperbacks, an imprint of HarperCollins, 2008), p. 65.

page 118   "This is the place that most makes me feel": Ibid, p. 316.

page 118   Move from a fear stance to a trust stance: Ibid, p. 213.

page 120   Booths are decorated festively: L.L. Barkat, "Marching Farmers, Homeless Slaves", *Christianity Today* <http://www.christianitytoday.com/ct/2008/novemberwebonly/148-21.0.html?start=2>.

page 121   "Treat each guest as though he or she were an angel": Adele Calhoun, *Spiritual Disciplines Handbook: Practices that Transform Us* (Downers Grove, Ill: InterVarsity Press, 2005), p. 140.

page 122   "Interconnectedness of God and life": Nanette Sawyer, *Hospitality: The Sacred Art... Discovering the Hidden Spiritual Power of Invitation and Welcome* (Woodstock, Vermont: Skylight Paths Publishing, 2008), p. 10.

page 122   "Is God the Force in the wind?": Ibid, p. 11.

page 123   "Posture of welcome" or "reverence": Ibid, p. 4.

page 124   "The completion of the circle of hospitality is generosity": Ibid, p. 4.

Epilogue

page 129   "Some people embarked on pilgrimage to major religious centers": Gerald L. Sittser, *Water from a Deep Well: Christian Spirituality from Early Martyrs to Modern Missionaries* (Downers Grove, Ill: InterVarsity Press, 2007), p. 152.

Gratitude

Many thanks to my dear family; you keep me smiling. To my girls especially, you bring poetry to my life (what a privilege) and to my husband, you keep me supplied in dark chocolate (and that too is a privilege!) Thanks to my mother and father who gave me so many beautiful things in life, in spite of the struggles. To Mom and Dad B, as always I have cherished your prayers. To my online community, you were at the beginning of this project, before it was even a project—your lively response to a series of posts on Wendell Berry's *The Gift of Good Land* was part of what sparked the idea for this book. Thanks to Marcus Goodyear for your kind and visionary editorial support. Glynn Young, you are my best self-assigned publicist and a marvelous partner in poetry crime. To my dear sister Sandi and my "sister" Ann Voskamp, how can I thank you for your tenacious belief in my writing and me? Laura Boggess, Sam Van Eman, Bradley J. Moore, Ann Kroeker, Gordon Atkinson, you are more than the people who work with me at *TheHighCalling.org*... you inspire me to great writing (and often to laughter). Christy Tennant and the people at International Arts Movement, you have embraced me beyond the book we did together (*InsideOut: poems*), supporting me as a writer and an artist and giving attention to projects like this, even though you aren't obliged to do so; you live your organizational vision. And I cannot end without saying this, "Thanks be to God."

Also from L.L. Barkat

Stone Crossings: Finding Grace in Hard and Hidden Places
(InterVarsity Press, 2008)

The only writer I know quite like L.L. Barkat is Eugene Peterson.
That probably tells you all you need to know.
—Scot McKnight, author of *The Blue Parakeet*

Stone Crossings shimmers grace...
—Gregory L. Jao, Regional Director, IVCF

... reminiscent of the prose of Annie Dillard...
—Monica Tenney, *Congregational Libraries Today*

InsideOut: poems (International Arts Movement, 2009)

Barkat is inviting us on a journey of awareness of hope.
—Makoto Fujimura, founder International Arts Movement

Of the calibre of Kenyon and Kooser, Barkat's writing is more than
mere words on a page; she gives you sight.
—Ann Voskamp, of Holy Experience

Beautiful, luminous poems... she's given us a gift here, a great gift.
—Glynn Young, Editor TweetspeakPoetry.com

To share about your 12-week journey, if you blog about it and would
like to request a possible link, please visit L.L. Barkat at
http://seedlingsinstone.blogspot.com.

Also from L.L. Barkat

Stone Crossings: Finding Grace in Hard and Hidden Places
(InterVarsity Press, 2008)

The only writer I know quite like L.L. Barkat is Eugene Peterson.
That probably tells you all you need to know.
—Scot McKnight, author of *The Blue Parakeet*

Stone Crossings shimmers grace...
—Gregory L. Jao, Regional Director, IVCF

... reminiscent of the prose of Annie Dillard...
—Monica Tenney, *Congregational Libraries Today*

InsideOut: poems (International Arts Movement, 2009)

Barkat is inviting us on a journey of awareness of hope.
—Makoto Fujimura, founder International Arts Movement

Of the calibre of Kenyon and Kooser, Barkat's writing is more than
mere words on a page; she gives you sight.
—Ann Voskamp, of Holy Experience

Beautiful, luminous poems... she's given us a gift here, a great gift.
—Glynn Young, Editor TweetspeakPoetry.com

To share about your 12-week journey, if you blog about it and would
like to request a possible link, please visit L.L. Barkat at
http://seedlingsinstone.blogspot.com.

Also from T. S. Poetry Press

Barbies at Communion: and Other Poems, by Marcus Goodyear

Marcus Goodyear's poems are portable, easily carried in the mind, tightly compressed and deceptively simple, like a capacious tent folded into a package you can tuck in your backpack.

— John Wilson, Editor, *Books & Culture*

A new zip-lock bag for Christian poetry holding gustiness and bravado.

— Diane Glancy, author *The Reason for Crows*

From Barbies to tea bags and credit cards, from broken pipes to communion wafers and mowing dead grass, Marcus Goodyear moves us through our world. His juxtapositions of the conventionally sacred and profane reveal to us the falsness of our conventions. Where the vision is large, all is sacred.

— John Leax, author *Tabloid News*

Marcus Goodyear's poems reveal a playful mind at work on the stuff of the world. Picking up something ordinary, he tilts it to show its wild friendship with mystery. He reveals Jesus hitching a ride in the back of a truck. He juxtaposes Higgs particles with a carnival. Even his credit card appears miraculous, talking, as it does, to "institutions of numbers."

— Jeanne Murray Walker, author *New Tracks, Night Falling*

Available online in e-book and print editions

Made in the USA
Lexington, KY
19 September 2011